LETTING GO OF
OF
Shame

About the authors:

Dr. Ronald T. Potter-Efron is a clinical psychotherapist. He has a M.S.W. from the University of Michigan and a Ph.D. in sociology from Purdue University. A former university professor, he specializes in the treatment of addictive disorders and anger and resentment counseling. He also is active in training professional counselors. He taught at an experimental college for eight years, and has trained in gestalt therapy techniques.

Patricia S. Potter-Efron is a family systems therapist and an individual and group therapist working mainly with families affected by chemical dependency. A graduate of Macalester College in St. Paul, she now directs Professional Growth Services, a program for adult children with dysfunctional families and does group work with recovering chemically dependent women.

The Potter-Efrons are co-editors of and contributors to *The Treatment of Shame and Guilt in Alcoholism Counseling* and *Aggression, Family Violence, and Chemical Dependency*, both published by Haworth Press. Ronald is also the author of *Shame, Guilt and Alcoholism: Treatment Issues in Clinical Practice*, published by Haworth.

LETTING GO OF
OF
Shame

UNDERSTANDING HOW SHAME AFFECTS YOUR LIFE

Ronald Potter-Efron
Patricia Potter-Efron

HAZELDEN®

INFORMATION & EDUCATIONAL SERVICES

First published October 1989.

ISBN: 0-89486-635-4

Library of Congress Catalog Card Number: 89-84784

Printed in the United States of America.

Editor's Note:
The stories in this book are composites of many individuals and their dealings with shame. Any resemblance to any one person is purely coincidental.

In the interest of fostering self-respect for each individual, regardless of gender, the authors have alternated gender references in this book — switching from "he" to "she." The authors believe the issues of shame know no boundaries in regard to sex, creed, color, or religious affiliation.

Contents

This book is dedicated to the memory of
C. Stanley Potter and Miles J. Efron.

ACKNOWLEDGMENTS

We would like to acknowledge those individuals who read and commented on this text as it gradually took shape: Denise Balduc, Paul Heck, Mark Morse, Jan and Richard Smith, and Lee Webster. Their comments proved quite useful in calling new or overlooked thoughts to our attention. Also, we thank Jennifer Potter-Efron for her excellent typing of the final draft. Judy Delaney was the editor at Hazelden whose enthusiastic support from the start both raised our spirits and kept us working. Finally, we want to share our appreciation for our many friends and associates who contributed their ideas and experiences of shame along with their warmth and caring.

Introduction - *A Definition of Shame*

Shame is an elusive concept. Although it has been studied periodically since the 1950s, it is far less well understood than its closest neighbor, guilt. Only recently have many books on shame begun to appear.

Some of the reasons for this neglect are historical accidents. For example, Sigmund Freud, the founder of psychoanalysis, happened to focus his attention on guilt rather than shame. Later, anthropologists thought that guilt was a higher level, more sophisticated feeling than shame. They assumed that advanced Western societies did not have or need shame.

Still, probably a better reason for shame's elusiveness is people's natural response to shame experiences: to hide and withdraw. The last thing most deeply shamed persons want to do is to talk about this feeling. They often conceal their shame even during therapy, preferring instead to discuss their anger, sadness, or fears. It is hard to admit feelings of shame. It is equally difficult to face others with that feeling. The result is that individuals become isolated from other people just when they need them the most — when they feel most disgraced and ashamed.

What is shame? It is more than a feeling. It is a set of physical responses (such as looking down or blushing) combined with predictable actions (such as hiding or withdrawing from others), uncomfortable thoughts (such as *I am a failure in life*), and spiritual despair. Our definition of *shame* is that it is a *painful belief in one's basic defectiveness as a human being.*

This book is divided into three sections. In the first section, we will attempt to grasp the shame experience by describing it carefully and by contrasting ordinary, constructive shame (shame you can use to improve your life) with the problems of excessive shame. Our basic belief is that shame can be a healthy and useful feeling (although painful). But it can also become unhealthy, especially when someone has too much of it. Deeply shamed persons suffer greatly. They cannot use their shame to improve their lives.

The second section covers the five different sources of shame:

- our genetic and biochemical makeup,
- our American culture,
- our families of origin,
- our current shaming relationships, and
- our own self-shaming thoughts and behaviors.

A person might be affected by any one or more of these influences. The important point is that there is no single source of shame that applies to everybody. Many badly shamed persons grew up with critical and unsupportive parents. Others are more influenced by shaming events in their adulthood, such as being married to a verbally abusive person. Still others' shame appears to come from a genetic predisposition, or their shame may reflect cultural bias and discrimination. Finally, certain persons are their own worst shamers. These people relentlessly attack themselves even when others try to support them.

We will learn guidelines for healing shame in the third section. Healing begins with understanding and is followed by action. Healing shame will require us to

- become fully aware of our shame,
- notice our defenses against shame,
- accept a certain amount of shame as part of the human condition,

- challenge shame, and
- set positive goals for ourselves to help replace our shame with self-worth.

When we start healing shame, we will be moving toward humanity, humility, autonomy, and competence. We'll be able to say, I am human, no better or worse than others, unique, and good enough as I am.

Exercises for your personal growth are located at the end of each chapter. We think these will be useful for you, particularly if you believe you have a significant problem with shame. Be sure to take your time with these exercises. You may want to begin a notebook where you can write your answers to the exercises, seeing just where shame is in your life and how you can turn bad shame into good shame. It might be a good idea to find someone you trust with whom you can discuss what you write down and think about.

We believe that you who are damaged by your shame can heal. You will need energy, patience, and persistence. You will also need understanding and courage. Above all, you will need hope — a deep faith that nobody needs to remain forever in personal despair. People who heal their shame discover they are freer to live lives that center around self-respect, dignity, honor, and realistic pride.

Shame and Guilt

Shame and guilt could be called the *interpersonal emotions*, because both tell us there is something wrong between us and the rest of the world. Both ask us to look at ourselves carefully and to make changes in our lives. Another similarity is that both shame and guilt can be valuable in moderation, but damaging when too strong. Too much of either emotion may be overwhelming.

There are important differences between shame and guilt. First, shame concerns a person's failure of *being*, while guilt points to a failure of *doing*. Shamed people believe something is basically wrong with them as human beings, while the guilty people believe they have done something wrong that must be corrected. Of course, a person could experience both shame and guilt at the same time. For example, the spouse who breaks his vow to be faithful may be full of remorse. He might say to himself that he has done something very bad — an admission of guilt. He might also believe he is weak, defective, or disgusting and that there must be something inherently wrong with him — all indicators of shame.

A second major difference is that the shamed people usually are bothered by their *shortcomings*, while guilty people notice their *transgressions*. People who are ashamed often see themselves as not being good enough, as failing to reach their goals in life. The shamed person thinks she is not as smart as her fellow workers, not as attractive as her mother, not as kind as her partner, not as interesting as her friends. By contrast, the guilty individual has gone too far, write Gerhart Piers and Milton Singer in their book, *Shame and Guilt*. She says to herself, *I wish I hadn't done that. I have harmed others, and I feel bad*.

The third difference between shame and guilt is that the shamed person fears *abandonment*, while the guilty person fears *punishment*. The reason the shamed person fears abandonment is that he believes he is too flawed to be wanted or valued by others. Someone who does not like or respect himself very much often expects others to leave him as soon as they realize he is less than perfect. The guilty person expects and fears punishment, because he has done something wrong and has to pay the price. The punishment might be as minor as a slap on the wrist or as great as a prison term.

Shame can be more difficult to heal than guilt, because it is about the person rather than specific actions. The shamed person heals by changing her self-concept so that she gains new self-respect and pride. Normally a slow and sometimes painful process, this involves looking deeply at our basic assumptions about our place in the universe.

Sometimes, the problems of shame and guilt blend into each other until it is almost impossible to distinguish between them. The person who begins with the question, "How could *I* have done something like *that?*" may be focusing attention on either the "that" or on the "I" part of the question. "How could I have done *that?*" implies a concern with behavior, transgression, and guilt. "How could *I* have done that?" implies a concern with identity, shortcomings, and shame. A person may very easily ask both halves of this question in sequence or even at the same time. Guilt leads toward shame and vice versa.

As a reader of this book, you may need to exercise patience. You naturally want relief from bad shame as quickly as possible. But as you read this book and think about shame, the problem may seem to be temporarily intensified. Stick with us. We will show you how to deal with bad shame, and how good, temporary shame is an important part of healthy living.

We have chosen to concentrate on the subject of shame in this book largely because so much less has been written about it than guilt, and because shame has been so poorly understood. Our focus will be on how you view yourself. Our goal is to help you learn to appreciate yourself more as valuable human beings with something important to contribute to the world.

SECTION ONE

UNDERSTANDING SHAME

Introduction

What is the shame experience like? How does ordinary, constructive shame differ from excessive and destructive shame?

In this section of the book, we will carefully describe why deeply shamed persons cannot improve their lives until they understand what shame is.

CHAPTER ONE

Shame: A Failure of the Whole Self

A two-year-old child explores the world. She finds a special place in the garden where she digs happily in the soft soil. She feels proud of her accomplishments. "Look at me," she wants to tell the world. "Look at what I can do. I am good."

"Just look at you!" shouts her mother. "Look at this mess. You are dirty. Your clothes are ruined. I'm very disappointed with you. You ought to be ashamed of yourself."

The child feels very small. She drops her head and stares at the ground. She sees her dirty hands and clothes and begins to feel dirty inside. She thinks there must be something very bad about her, something so bad she will never really be clean. She hears her mother's disdain. She feels defective.

* * * * * * * * * *

A young woman, age sixteen, has recently begun dating. Her boyfriend seems to be a gentleman, and, indeed, he never tries to force her to do anything she doesn't like. She gradually trusts him more and more. They pass romantic notes back and forth during classes.

He affectionately names her "Sexy Girl" in these notes.

One day as she walks through school, her boyfriend's buddy shouts as she passes: "Hey, Sexy Girl, how you doing?" She suddenly realizes that her boyfriend must have shown their notes to others. She feels instantly humiliated. Her face burns with embarrassment. She wants to run away. She feels that everyone can see right through her.

Later, she gets a call from her boyfriend. He wants to apologize for what happened. But by now she has become furious. "Get away from me!" she cries. "I can never forgive you for what you did. I'll never talk with you again!"

* * * * * * * * * *

A middle-aged man has a secure job with a small firm. His chances for advancement seem excellent, and he consistently gets positive work reviews from his supervisor. He knows that he is well-regarded by his peers.

One day his boss criticizes this man for a small mistake. Perhaps he was late to a meeting; maybe he forgot to send along an invoice with an order. Very little damage was done. His employer simply calls the problem to this man's attention without attacking him.

Still, the man feels utterly defeated. He "knows" something is basically wrong with him. He believes he has been exposed as a fraud. He is certain that others will recognize that he should not even be allowed to work there anymore. He is not perfect, so he must be worthless. He spends hours remembering every mistake he has ever made at this and previous jobs, which only makes him feel worse. He retreats to his office, closes the door, and hides there the rest of the day. He knows he will never be good enough.

* * * * * * * * * *

An older man spends much of his time criticizing everybody around him. His wife is stupid; his son is lazy; his daughter is foolish; his friends are crude; the world is rotten. He does not hesitate to tell others that he is smarter, more sensible, and just generally better than they. He advertises his sense of superiority. He expects to be honored.

Perhaps a few people buy his image. But others recognize that this man is wearing a mask. They see through his pomposity and arrogance to the insecure and flawed person inside. They realize that this man tries to convince the world that he is better than others, when he really feels he is worse. Still, living around this man is quite difficult, since he is so contemptuous of others. Rather than honoring or worshipping him, they pull away, avoiding him and hesitating to tell him anything about themselves.

* * * * * * * * * *

The four persons in these examples have one thing in common — the feeling of shame. Shame is a painful feeling that can be felt throughout your body. It has many variations and never looks exactly alike in any two individuals. The little girl's shame, for example, is much more physical and less intellectual than the older man's. The teenage girl's immediate sense of exposure and humiliation contrasts with the businessman's long-term doubts. The older man hides his shame from himself more than from others, while the businessman has kept his shame a complete secret. Only the teenage girl in these examples converted her shame into rage.

The shame experience does have common features: definite and strong physical responses, uncomfortable thoughts, troublesome behaviors, and spiritual agony.

11

The Physical Component of Shame

The sudden feeling of strong shame is an overpowering experience. One moment earlier we seemed fine, full of energy, self-worth, and joy. Then something bad happens, perhaps something as trivial as noticing a stain on our shirt or blouse, perhaps something more obvious like our boss yelling at us about a mistake. These are times when we would like to stay cool and composed. We would love to be able to respond to these situations with dignity, grace, and poise.

If only our bodies would cooperate. Instead, we feel our faces getting warm. For some reason, we cannot force our eyes to look forward, because they insist on following as our head bends toward the ground. Maybe our chest becomes heavy. Our heart might pound as we sense that, right now, we are not in control of our body. Some of us may feel an empty sensation in our gut. Time may seem to crawl as we writhe in the grip of acute self-consciousness. We can barely talk. We are ashamed.

It's bad enough to feel this first round of shame. But once we notice these sensations, we may begin to feel even worse. We become ashamed of our shame. We may desperately try to tell ourselves to calm down, but our bodies still refuse to listen. Warmth turns into heat, and we blush with embarrassment. Now our eyes are driven down, and we have to fight a compelling urge to retreat, to turn our backs on the entire situation. We may start to feel nauseated. We are becoming sick with our shame.

Not all shame attacks are this painful. But shame is almost always a physical event. Its more subtle forms include brief hesitations in speech, glancing away while talking, delicate shifts of conversation, and barely noticeable feelings of facial warmth and discomfort. Shame is, above all, a feeling.

Two other physical responses are common during a shame attack. First, we start to feel smaller and smaller. Second, the persons around us seem to get bigger, louder, and more dangerous. It is as if we were shrinking. What may be happening is that we have pulled inward, instinctively taking up less room by contracting our arms and legs. We are trying to protect ourselves by making ourselves feel small. People who experience this report that they feel like young children when they feel shame.

Shamed people feel open, vulnerable, and exposed to others despite this effort to shrink down. This is more than a thought — it is a bodily response that can be very uncomfortable. Another person's look seems to almost touch them. Skin seems to become transparent so that others can see right through them. The shamed person would dearly like to become completely invisible. Instead, this person feels totally open for inspection.

But shame is more than a feeling. Disconcerting feelings trigger painful thoughts, usually all too familiar thoughts that increase the shamed person's troubles. These thoughts confirm the shamed person's feeling of having something to feel ashamed about.

Thoughts About Shame

Shame produces such powerful feelings that it is easy to underestimate the importance of our thoughts in recording, labeling, and even increasing that emotion. Scholars often write that shame is much more physical than guilt — that guilt occurs in our heads, while shame occurs in our bodies. There is some truth to this argument. Shamed people usually feel so bad that they do not want to dwell on the experience. They want to get rid of these feelings as soon as possible. Who would want to think about their shame?

And yet, shame is also very much a mental process. We do think about shame, and sometimes we cannot stop thinking about our embarrassments, defeats, and humiliations. We end up calling ourselves terrible names ("Dummy," "Idiot," "Bitch," et cetera) that add to our shame. Self-hatred develops in this manner, one insult at a time.

Here are thoughts that shamed people commonly tell themselves:

- I am defective (damaged, broken, a mistake, flawed).
- I am dirty (soiled, ugly, unclean, impure, filthy, disgusting).
- I am incompetent (not good enough, inept, ineffectual, useless).
- I am unwanted (unloved, unappreciated, uncherished).
- I deserve to be abandoned (forgotten, unloved, left out).
- I am weak (small, impotent, puny, feeble).
- I am bad (awful, dreadful, evil, despicable).
- I am pitiful (contemptible, miserable, insignificant).
- I am nothing (worthless, invisible, unnoticed, empty).
- I deserve criticism (condemnation, disapproval, destruction).
- I feel ashamed (embarrassed, humiliated, mortified, dishonored).

Persons who are deeply shamed have these thoughts with great regularity. In fact, they often assume that almost everybody thinks this way — that most people view themselves as fundamentally bad, flawed, and shameful. They are also pretty sure that others agree with their self-evaluation. They believe their family and associates see them as defective too. People who are deeply shamed expect ridicule and disdain from everyone because they believe they deserve condemnation. If, by chance, they receive praise instead of criticism, they are likely to reject both the praise (*If only they knew how badly I've really done on this job*) and the praiser (*She is just making fun of me by pretending to like what I do*).

These negative thoughts compound shame. They tell the people who have them that they have been shamed, should be shamed, can't escape the shame, and will always be ashamed. They tell the shamed people that they are different from others.

Shamed Actions

What actions does the shamed person take to get rid of

shame? How can the suffering be alleviated? We'll discuss negative responses to shame here. Positive responses — what can be done to turn shame into power — will be discussed in Section Three. Responses to shame a person may have include paralysis, faltering energy, escapism, withdrawal, perfectionism, criticism, and rage. We will discuss each of these here.

Paralysis. The shamed person may be paralyzed, unable to do anything. The person may want to speak back to an accuser, but no words come to mind. He may want to run away, but he cannot mobilize enough energy to do so. He is stuck. His paralysis intensifies his shame, because now he can attack himself for not being strong enough to stand up for himself.

Faltering energy. Shame steals energy just as it diminishes self-worth. Most people slowly crumble in the face of a shaming attack. They feel smaller, weaker, less potent. They are diminished.

Escapism. The shamed person usually wants badly to escape. She feels overwhelmed in the current social situation. Like the businessman and the adolescent girl in the examples, most shamed persons will attempt to withdraw from others. They seek out private, secure places — places where nobody can see them in their shame. Deeply shamed people may become very private people who prefer to spend their time alone.

Withdrawal. This can be more subtle than simply running away. Sometimes, people develop elaborate masks to cover their real selves. They smile a lot, always try to please others, and appear self-confident and comfortable. Convinced that others would despise them if they could see past their masks to their real selves, people who are shamed try to keep their shame a secret. They withdraw emotionally.

Perfectionism. The shamed person may also reason that she will have nothing to feel ashamed about if she never makes a mistake. She then becomes a perfectionist. But she is caught in the trap of being human. Human beings make mistakes, but to her any error advertises her shame. She cannot afford to be human. She cannot afford to fall short in anything she does.

Criticism. Shamed people often become highly critical of everyone else. They seem eager to point out the weaknesses of those around them, just like the older man did in the chapter-opening example. This behavior is like the magician who suddenly pulls his coin from behind the ear of a member of the audience.

"Abracadabra!" he says. "What was mine is now yours."

"Abracadabra!" says the perpetual critic. "I give my shame to you." Not only does the critic rid herself of these bad feelings, she can also actually believe that she is better than anyone else. She may need to feel superior to avoid being submerged in inferiority feelings.

Rage. This is another response to shame. One way to fight against humiliation is to attack the supposed attacker. The rageful person may become furious with another, sometimes over the slightest affront to his dignity. For example, he may rail against the host who forgets his name, the spouse who says hello to an old high school acquaintance, "authorities" just because they have power, and his children for wanting attention. Those who combine shame with rage may become verbally or physically abusive. By attacking the personalities of others, they defend their own fragile identities.

Shame: A Spiritual Crisis

Shame involves a failure of the total being. The person who is shamed believes that she should not exist. It is not that she has *done* something wrong (that is guilt). The shamed person believes that she *is* something wrong. She is a shame, not just ashamed.

The shamed person encounters a spiritual crisis at his very core. Does he have any right even to exist? Is he some dreadful mistake that nobody would claim? Would even God forsake him? Is he unworthy of love? When shame is strongest, many people would answer yes to each of these questions.

Shame temporarily deprives us of our humanness. We begin

to think of ourselves as subhuman, less than fully alive. We lose the sense of communion with others. We lose our connections with a Higher Power, so that we become isolated from all external sources of comfort. We can feel a tremendous loneliness at the center of our being.

The shamed person feels worthless: worth less than everyone around her, worth nothing. She sees herself as a debit to others, a problem in their lives. She may hope that others will tolerate her, but she sees no possibility that they would want to embrace her. During moments of strong shame, she can think of nothing about herself that is worthwhile. She may consider suicide.

A feeling of emptiness accompanies feelings of worthlessness. The shamed person often feels hollowed out. He seems to be a "nothing." He has no identity of his own. He wears a mask both to cover his shame and to hide his emptiness. He has lost his soul to his shame.

Shamed persons sometimes appear to be quite arrogant. They act as if they were badly overinflated balloons, so swollen with pride that they float above the earth. But no amount of ego-inflation can undo the damage from shame. These persons are still empty inside. They can attempt to conceal the sense of nothingness that comes with deep shame, but it remains until it can be addressed honestly.

Summary

Shame has many components. It is first a painful feeling that involves the face, the entire body. Uncomfortable thoughts precede, accompany, and follow these physical feelings. A shamed individual may be too paralyzed to act. If she can, she will usually withdraw from others either physically or emotionally. A shamed person also suffers a spiritual crisis in which she feels less than human and cut off from others as well as her Higher Power.

EXERCISES

Exercise One

Compare your experiences of shame to those of the four people in the descriptions at the beginning of the chapter. Write your answers on a separate sheet of paper.

1. Has someone's sudden, critical, or harsh response left you feeling like a bad person, even though what you had done was innocent? What happened?
2. Have you felt betrayed or embarrassed by someone? Did you respond by withdrawing, getting angry, or both? What happened? How did you feel about yourself then?
3. Have you been very critical of yourself, even though you had made only an insignificant mistake? What happened? What names did you call yourself? What did you decide about your self-worth?
4. Have you ever found yourself criticizing another person, pointing out to yourself (and maybe to the person) how much better it is to be like you than like him or her? Have you criticized others more often when you are unhappy with yourself? Have you noticed that some of the faults you have criticized in others remind you of your own behaviors or thoughts?

Exercise Two

Take a minute to examine the physical sensations you connect to shame. Remember a time when you felt smaller than life, or when you felt looked at, looked through, or exposed. Allow yourself to remember some of the feelings you had then. Where did your eyes look? What did your hands do? How did your face feel? Your stomach? Were you warm or cool? Now take three deep breaths, in and out, and as you exhale each breath let these feelings drain down out of you and into the floor. Describe what you feel.

Exercise Three

When you feel shame, how does it affect your self-esteem? Take note of each statement that is similar to thoughts or ideas you experience when you feel ashamed.

- I have no right to exist.
- I am inadequate.
- Something is wrong with me.
- I am not worth loving.
- I am a mistake.
- I don't belong.
- I deserve to be abandoned.
- I am ugly.
- I am dirty.
- I am a burden to others.
- I don't count.
- I am nothing.
- I deserve criticism.
- I am unwanted.
- I am worthless.
- I am dishonored.
- I am not good enough.
- I am humiliated.
- I should not be.

Each of these statements makes it harder to feel that you fit into and play a useful part in the world.

Now write three things that are good about you. List those things you know are good about you, or things other people, who can see you more objectively, tell you are good about yourself. Remember, feelings of shame create painful ideas and attitudes about ourselves THAT ARE OFTEN NOT TRUE.

CHAPTER TWO

When Shame Is Good

"That's one day I will never forget. I thought I was the best athlete in the whole world when I won the regional and made state. I felt humiliated when I didn't even place in the finals. But now, when I look back, I'm almost glad I lost. I learned that day that I would have to work hard to do something with my life. Up till then I had a free ride."

* * * * * * * * * *

He could bear the shame no longer. Every day his wife told him that he was a failure in his career and a lousy father as well. He had begun to dread even coming home. He felt more and more like a failure. Finally, he realized that he had to listen to his shame. He needed to confront the problems in his marriage, or he would never get rid of that terrible sick feeling in his gut.

* * * * * * * * * *

She had an excellent job as a factory manager. Her future seemed assured. Unfortunately, her shame kept nagging at her. "You know this is not what you want to be doing with your life," it seemed to say. "You are selling yourself short by not completing your education."

* * * * * * * * * *

"I used to eat all the time when I felt bad. I ran away from my feelings, especially my shame. Now, I realize that my shame is part of me. Instead of running from it, I take the time to listen to what my body is trying to tell me. I'm less afraid of shame than before."

* * * * * * * * * *

The term *good shame* may sound like a contradiction. *What good can come from this basically uncomfortable feeling?* we may ask ourselves. We need to realize shame can have great value, as long as we are not overwhelmed by it. The person who experiences shame becomes acutely aware of who he is and the boundary between himself and others. Carl Schneider writes in *Shame, Exposure and Privacy* that there would be no sense of privacy or intimacy without shame. Shame also promotes humanity, humility, autonomy, and competence. Certain shame feelings can be good in the same way that anger, sadness, and fear — painful emotions — tell us something is very wrong in our life and motivate us to do something to change.

Excessive shame is *bad shame*. Excessive shame can trap a person in a cage of self-hatred, despair, and worthlessness. It can drive people away from each other so relationships are damaged or abandoned. Excessive shame leads to paralysis when someone says to himself, *I am so defective that I will never get better. I might as well give up.*

Not enough shame is also *bad shame*. People who are shame-deficient don't have a very clear idea of who they are. They have little understanding of anybody's need for boundaries. Intimacy is difficult because it demands privacy and modesty, both of which people who are shame-deficient are missing or have in short supply.

Good shame, by contrast, is a *temporary* state that tells us something is seriously wrong in our relationship with the world. It tells us that the connection between us and other people is broken and needs fixing. Good shame is like having a true friend, one who is not afraid to tell you that you are messing up your life. A good friend may sometimes have to tell you the truth, even when that truth is painful to both of you. This friend demonstrates her love and respect for you by sticking with you during troubled times. She shows her courage by confronting problems before they become unsolvable.

We can use our shame constructively when we develop the ability to listen to the important messages we receive along with the shame. Some of these messages are:

- "You are not living up to your goals right now. Is there anything you can do differently so you would feel better?"
- "You are feeling exposed and vulnerable now. Make sure you can trust these people."
- "You feel like you are not good enough. What is going on with you right now?"

These are valuable communications that should not be ignored. But they are temporary messages. Good shame tells us that something is wrong now and invites us to examine our life and perhaps change our thoughts or actions. The person who can listen to, and act on, his shame instead of running away from it will eventually feel better about himself. The payoff is that the person who makes friends with his shame will gradually gain more self-respect.

Good Shame and Self-Awareness

Shame is a great teacher. The person who feels a moment of shame can learn much about himself and about others. For example, the man in Chapter One who withered in the face of his employer's minor criticism discovered that he doubts his own *right* to be a successful businessman.

The shamed person is self-conscious. She is aware of her appearance, mannerisms, habits, and expressions. She watches and judges herself even while she wonders what others are thinking about her. Like the adolescent who spends hours in front of the mirror, the shamed person scrutinizes herself for flaws. She may become aware of a wide variety of shortcomings not only in her looks, but more importantly in her actions and in her relationships with others. A shamed person can use this knowledge to change what she says and does.

Shame is an uncomfortable feeling. That is why people who are not paralyzed by their shame will utilize it to alter their behavior. Some of these changes may be relatively small, such as avoiding future embarrassment by wearing more appropriate clothing to a social gathering. But shame also brings much more serious matters to our attention.

- The person who realizes with shame that he has chosen the wrong career must face a bitter truth so that he can get on with his life.
- The person who feels spiritually empty may be able to transform this into a quest for a new and deeper religious experience.

One theme we have noticed in working with people in our therapy practice: *shame must be faced courageously for it to be useful.* The person who is terrified of her shame and only wants to avoid it gains nothing from shame except fear and pain. The person who will stand up to her shame grows right through her discomfort into a richer and more meaningful awareness of who she is and what she is doing on this planet.

Since shame is about feeling we are complete failures, not just about one or two actions we have taken, it is easy to become discouraged and pessimistic when dealing with shame issues. Shame can be difficult to change because it strikes at the very core of a person's existence. It can be quite tenacious. But shame does not have to be a permanent condition. The person who pays careful attention to his shame without being completely intimidated by it will find tremendous value in that temporary state. Shame can be paired with hope just as well as with despair.

Good Shame and Relationships

The overly shamed person often believes that something is basically wrong in the way he relates to others. He thinks that he deserves disapproval. He feels socially defective. When he compares himself with others, he tends only to notice his weaknesses. He probably sees himself as less intelligent, handsome, and attractive than he really is. The extremely shamed person becomes continually conscious of such shortcomings.

But good shame is moderate and temporary. Most persons will feel this type of shame when a problem arises between themselves and at least one other person. This feeling of shame may be necessary for someone to realize that she is in trouble. Again, good shame leads toward self-awareness, which then promotes effective work in relationships.

Shame Can Motivate Personal Change

Shame issues may be small or great in scope. It may be no big deal when a person suddenly recognizes that he has been making a fool of himself by joking around too often. Or it may be a big deal. He may realize that all his life he has invited attention through acts of self-humiliation. His sudden shame about this behavior is a sign that he wants to change. This temporary shame may help him eventually face the world with dignity and self-respect.

The potential to feel shame is always present in our relationships with others. That feeling of shame may tell a person to retreat from a relationship, long enough for her to try to understand what has gone wrong. The shame experience might even force someone to question the value of maintaining a relationship. For example, if almost every time a woman meets another person and she comes away full of shame, she may recognize that the relationship is fundamentally flawed. Relationships that center around shame are unhealthy. Those that cannot be converted to focus on mutual respect and dignity may have to be severed for the sake of both parties.

Shaming Patterns Can Be Corrected

Most relationships occasionally drift into shaming patterns. One partner will call the other a name; the other responds by pointedly ignoring the comment. The shame that either or both persons experience acts as a clear signal that the relationship has been damaged. The message in its simplest form is this: "What has just happened has triggered my shame. Let's stop before we hurt each other more."

Shame carries with it a sense of urgency. The shamed individual will be strongly motivated to do something to feel better. Relationships in which both partners are sensitive to shame will be improved in the long run when the partners attend carefully to each other's pain.

Shame can act paradoxically. At first, the shamed person usually wants to run away from others. But, ultimately, the shamed person seeks connection with others. He feels disconnected, yet hopes somehow to return to the warmth of family and friends. Good shame guides the outcast back into the community.

Good Shame as a Guideline for Living

Shame is a powerful but manageable experience for most persons. But there is much more to shame than simply surviving it. Moderate shame can help people discover (and rediscover) important truths about life.

Four of these truths are the principles of humanity, humility, autonomy, and competence.

- *The principle of humanity:* Each person belongs to the human race — no person is totally shameful and subhuman, or a god different from everyone else.
- *The principle of humility:* No person is intrinsically better or worse than anyone else.
- *The principle of autonomy:* Each person has some control over his or her own actions, but very little over the behavior of others.

- *The principle of competence:* Each person can strive to be "good enough" without having to be perfect or a shame-based failure.

This material will be described in more detail later in the book. For now, we just want to emphasize that *shame can have great value.* What person could ever discover her basic sense of humanity if she succeeded in everything she did? What person could accept the limits of the human condition if she never experienced embarrassment? Shame consistently deflates egos before people get so inflated with pride and arrogance that they lose contact with other people.

Good Shame and a Sense of Humor Go Hand in Hand

If we can laugh at ourselves, we can gain from our shame. Can we see the irony when a mere human being begins to see himself either as God's greatest gift to the species, or as the lowliest worm that ever slithered through the mud?

Here is an example from our lives of the value of shame. A few years ago, Ron was asked to attend an "important" meeting at the university where he taught. He put on his best suit in the morning and left for the campus. By the time he got to the stairs leading to the meeting room, he was full of self-importance. Loaded with false pride, he jogged up, hoping a lot of people were noticing him right then. His head began to lift upward to reflect his feelings of superiority. Perhaps that is why he tripped on the stairs and crashed to the floor.

As Ron was on his way to the floor, he thought, *I hope nobody is watching me now!* What a contrast. The moment before, he wanted everyone to pay attention to him. Now he fervently wished for invisibility. His sudden shame made him feel *temporarily* like the biggest fool on earth.

Without humor, this "fall from glory" could have been disastrous. A person who is deeply shamed might think this accident proves that he is really a bad person who deserves to be humiliated in public. But Ron believes that the message for him in this incident is that he is neither as great as he would like to be, nor as awful as he feels when he embarrasses himself with his clumsiness. He is simply human.

Summary

We all face shame in one form or another. Shame is neither always good nor always bad. The important thing is what we do with our shame. When shame is recognized, accepted, and used to investigate our relationship with ourselves and with others, it is a beneficial feeling. Moderate shame promotes self-awareness and an appreciation of relationships. It can act as a guideline for leading meaningful and rich lives.

Some shame is necessary for us to develop into contributing members of society. Shame is most helpful when we receive it in small or moderate doses that do not overwhelm us with despair. Good shame needs to be embraced rather than avoided, and welcomed rather than feared. We need to learn how to become friends with this shame.

Unfortunately, many things can go wrong in the arena of shame. Overwhelming shame can damage the individual almost beyond repair, and lack of shame can leave a person without human warmth. These issues will be discussed in the next chapters.

EXERCISES

Exercise One

When Ron fell on the stairs, he was reminded that he is simply human, and not the most important person in the world. He also learned that he needs a sense of humor to keep his actions in perspective. Have you ever had a similar experience, one that helped you realize that you are no better and no worse than any other person? Write it down.

Exercise Two

Susan argued with Greg. Instead of being fair, she tried to shame Greg into doing what she wanted, telling him he was "stupid" and "selfish" to have his own thoughts and opinions on the matter. Later, Susan felt ashamed of calling Greg names and trying to manipulate him. This "good shame" helped Susan recognize that she needed to change her behavior. Have you ever shamed someone by calling the person names or putting him or her down? How did this behavior lead you to feel about yourself? How could you have used good shame to have altered your behavior? Write about your experience.

Exercise Three

Bob painted his shed in a hurry. He just wanted to get it over with. But when he looked at it later, he could see the paint was uneven. What's more, he'd splashed white paint on the red trim in many places and smeared the shed windows and doorknob with red paint. Instead of feeling relieved to get the job done, he felt ashamed of how it looked. His slapdash job just wasn't good enough — it wasn't up to his standards.

He used his feelings of shame to motivate himself to even up the coat of paint, repair the splash damage on the trim, and wash the windows and doorknob. When he was done, he felt pleased with the job he had done. Have you ever had the experience of benefiting from your shame in a similar kind of way? Write it down.

CHAPTER THREE

Excessive Shame: The Shame-Based Person

A thirty-year-old woman has seen three counselors in the last five years. Her complaint each time has been the same. "No matter what I do, no matter what I read or who I talk to, I just feel totally worthless. I'm certain that no one could ever love me because I have no good qualities. I feel like a complete failure in life. I hate myself."

* * * * * * * * *

A middle-aged man has almost no identity of his own. He tries to please everyone he meets, to become whatever they want him to be. He wears a mask of pleasantness so well that even he has no idea what would happen if he took it off. He thinks that if people were to see through his mask, they would discover that he is worthless or disgusting. They might not want to ever speak with him again.

* * * * * * * * *

Chronic, relentless shame is devastating. This shame is unlike the normal, healthy shame described in the last chapter. People who are shame-based have become stuck in their shame. Mired in feelings of worthlessness, defectiveness, and despair, they are full of doubt about their validity as human beings. They judge themselves mercilessly and often try to be perfect in a desperate attempt to hold off their shame.

How do some persons become shame-based? The most honest answer is that nobody knows exactly what traps these individuals in their shame. Certainly, many persons grow up in families in which put-downs, personal attacks, and the threat of abandonment are commonplace events. Others find themselves as adults caught in shaming relationships with spouses or with bosses and slowly lose their sense of self-esteem. Whatever the historical or immediate sources of shame, people who are shame-based have learned to shame themselves repeatedly. The person who is shame-based usually believes that others despise him. The key, however, is that he despises himself more than anyone else is capable of doing.

We will explore the many sources of shame in a later section of this book. The purpose of this chapter is to describe the behavior and thoughts of the person who is shame-based. We will also note several mechanisms that the person who is shame-based uses in order to survive.

The World of the Person Who Is Shame-Based

The person who is shame-based sees herself as deeply and permanently flawed. She "knows" she is not like other persons. She "knows" she is different. She "knows" she is so bad she is beyond repair. She "knows" she is less than fully human. She "knows" she will never be allowed to join others in a world of love, respect, and pride.

This person is stuck in her shame. She doesn't see shame as a temporary state, something that can help a person learn and grow. She believes that her shame is an irreversible and endless condition. She believes that her fate in life is to suffer shame, that she is essentially defective.

This person has created a myth about herself and the world.

In this myth, there are only good or bad people, black or white truths, and absolute certainties. This is a painful world since she believes that her fate is certain. She believes that she will live and die with shame. She may fight from time to time to escape her shame. She may yearn to gain a sense of dignity and worth. But the person who is deeply shamed frequently discovers that she cannot leave her world of shame for very long. Her shame mercilessly calls her back and demands her loyalty.

Shattering the Myth that You Must Live with Constant Shame

We call this situation a myth because nobody has to live forever in shame. There is room enough for everyone in this world. There is no such thing as a subhuman human. The wonderful thing about shame, even excessive shame, is that people can learn to live with it and grow spiritually richer in the process. But the person who is deeply shamed must learn how to challenge his belief that he is intrinsically valueless. Shame-based persons become accustomed to interpreting events from the perspective of disgrace. They need to discover how to see the world from a less threatening perspective. They need to challenge and discard their own myth that dooms them to a life of feeling shame. For instance, the woman at the start of this chapter will need to accept her positive characteristics, while the man with virtually no identity will need to find courage to take off his mask so that he can discover his true self.

How We Tend to See Ourselves

Persons who are shame-based are quite critical of themselves. They can always find something to criticize about their appearance, behavior, or personality. They set such high standards for themselves that they can never get close to reaching them. When they inevitably fail (*Three A's and a B may be good enough for others, but to me that proves I'm a failure*), they call themselves all kinds of terrible names.

Persons who are shame-based are also very self-conscious. Hypersensitive to criticism, they are always alert to the possibility of humiliation. They expect to be judged by others, since they spend so much effort condemning themselves. Because they can only attend to the deficits that others notice in them, they often dread formal events such as annual performance reviews at work. They simply do not hear a combination of praise and criticism as a balanced mixture. While they accept criticism as deserved, they regard whatever praise they receive as phony or misguided. They compare themselves frequently with their friends, partners, and peers; the problem is that they usually focus on how they are inadequate, and not on the fact that they are as good as others.

Persons who are shame-based may unconsciously seek relationships that confirm their shame. People who think they are basically worthless are easy prey to those who gain their self-worth by attacking others. *I know my lover is mean to me, but who else would want me?* they may ask themselves. Their excessive shame sets them up to be humiliated in their most important relationships.

Few persons suffer all the pain we have described here. Most people, even those with an excess of shame, can experience periods of honor and dignity. Few persons are so deeply shamed that they never feel good about themselves. Additionally, many persons who normally deal well with their shame can go through periods where they become swamped with shame. At those times, they might feel many of the effects of shame we've described, but eventually return to a more positive state.

Still, many persons do respond to the world from a shame-based perspective. This means that they expect to be shamed, seek out shaming experiences that confirm this expectation, and regularly shame themselves with excessive criticism. They live in a world of shame.

Shame Spirals

Normal shame occurs in *waves* that can be powerful, but are limited in how long they last. A person will feel ashamed, lose energy, and perhaps temporarily withdraw from others. But that person usually can recover fairly quickly, perhaps even learning from his pain new ways to rebuild a connection between himself and others.

Shame needs immediate attention. One reason for this is that shame *waves* can easily turn into shame *spirals*. These spirals are like whirlpools that spin faster and faster. They can last as long as several months, during which a person painfully reviews her shame and feels increasingly worse about herself.

In a typical shame spiral, a person might become aware of a shortcoming. It could be trivial such as forgetting to make a phone call. Perhaps suddenly embarrassed, this person has shameful thoughts and feelings. This is immediate shame. He may withdraw from the situation to regain his composure. So far, this is perfectly normal. He will be fine if he takes time to address his shame and takes positive steps to deal with it.

But serious problems can develop at this point, particularly if he is shame-based. Current shame can trigger recollections of past shame. That is why it is difficult to feel a "little" shame. Once a person starts to feel shame, it can quickly become excruciating. The spiral can accelerate as a person remembers other times when he felt shame. He becomes flooded with uncomfortable and scary thoughts.

By now he may doubt his value as a human being. His shame seems permanent. His ability to appreciate times when he felt healthy pride and self-respect diminishes.

This signals the need for a general retreat from situations that could increase the shame. For instance, a person who initially avoided someone who said things that bothered her won't go to the building where that person works. The person who feels shamed becomes more vigilant, needing to guard against exposure of her shame.

The shame spiral continues when the person feels shame about being ashamed. *If I were half a man, I would not have to feel like this*, he thinks. By now, he cannot stand the thought of facing anybody. He has fallen into isolation and isolates himself — physically, emotionally, and spiritually.

Survival Strategies for Persons Who Are Deeply Shamed

Most people can stand up to normal, temporary shame. That kind of shame certainly hurts, but it will eventually disappear. Good shame provides messages we need to hear. But, for the person who lives with excessive shame, shame never seems to go away, no matter what she does. If she listened to it all the time, she might be driven to take desperate action or just to give up in despair. This extreme shame often seems too painful to endure.

There are several ways people distort their shame feelings. The person who represses shame may not even be aware that she is defending herself against feelings of shame. She may not even recognize shame as the problem.

Defenses against shame may help the person deal with self-hatred and pain, but in the long run they do not heal shame. No one can learn to benefit from shame by ignoring it. Defenses against shame are survival strategies only; shame-based individuals who use them cannot learn that they are valuable persons who are worthy of love and respect.

Denial

The first kind of defense is *denial*. Someone who is in denial simply stays unaware of her shame. She deceives herself into believing she has no shame, when, in fact, she would experience great shame if she were fully aware of what was happening inside. She badly wants to believe she is completely acceptable to herself and to others, and so she blinds herself to whatever would bring her shame.

The person who is shame-based often lives in a world of appearances. He will do anything to protect his image as a good person, even if that means ignoring reality. For example, many alcoholics deny their drinking problem. They would feel tremendous shame if they admitted they couldn't control their alcohol use. They believe something must be wrong with anyone who is powerless over a mere bottle. They cannot understand how someone could be both an alcoholic and a good person at the same time. They believe: *An alcoholic is a worthless bum. I'm not that way. I'd hate myself if I were a drunk. I can't be an alcoholic.* Their fear of overwhelming shame is so strong they are blinded to the evidence of addiction. These persons cannot face their shame, so they convince themselves there is no problem.

Denial of shame is not exclusive to alcoholics. After all, shame threatens the core identity of a person. One person may "forget" about sexual behavior or desires that she believes are shameful. Another person believes it is shameful that her mother stutters or her son is mentally retarded because she perceives these things as defects. Still another person denies the seemingly trivial fact that he is losing hair, or that he can no longer run as fast because, to him, aging is a shameful process. Whatever could bring shame to someone can be defended with denial. We deny what we dare not see.

Living in denial takes its toll on a person. We can ignore reality, but that doesn't make it go away. The alcoholic who insists there is no problem may die from his disease. The woman who is humiliated by her mother's stuttering may remain forever cut off from her mother's love. The person who feels shame about aging may be unable to respect himself for who and what he is. These people would gain much by facing reality, but they can only do that when they learn that they can survive their shame.

Withdrawal

Another survival strategy against shame is *withdrawal*. People withdraw when they have been touched by shame, and personal contact with others is too painful to handle. Flight is a normal reaction to situations when people feel exposed and vulnerable.

A high school student, for instance, is given the assignment of making a short speech in front of his class. Unfortunately, he starts off poorly, stammering and losing his concentration. His classmates laugh at him. Now all he can think about is getting away as fast as he can. He wants to run from the room before he is overwhelmed with humiliation. He feels utterly defeated. The student might tell himself that he will never do anything in front of others again. Even years later, as an adult, he may shy away from opportunities that would involve speaking in public. If he does have to speak to a group, he may fail again because he is already convinced he will only make a fool of himself. He has learned to associate being visible with shame.

Withdrawal is a common reaction to shame. Remember that the initial physical reaction to shame is to break eye contact and look down or aside. A person who is shamed more or less says to her companions: *Right now I feel so bad about myself that I cannot look you in the eye. I can't stay close to you because that will only increase my shame.* Already feeling naked before the world, a person who is shamed certainly doesn't want another person to stare at her. She believes, at least temporarily, that everyone can see her soul, see that she is inadequate and bad.

Persons who are shamed also withdraw in other ways. Perhaps they evade uncomfortable topics of conversation or stay emotionally unavailable to others. Some persons practice the art of low visibility. They are always there, but not visible. One example is the very talented person behind the scenes who is so afraid of exposure that she lets others take credit for her accomplishments.

A person who is shame-based can become trapped in this withdrawal from others. He may do anything to keep others distant, as if he had already been shamed by them. Direct, meaningful, or intimate connections to others are very threatening to people who do not feel good about themselves. They are protecting themselves from the humiliation of being judged.

Rage

What happens when a person who is deeply shamed cannot withdraw from a threatening situation? *Rage,* another survival strategy against shame, is a likely response. The rageful person is shouting a warning: *Don't get any closer! You are getting too near my shame, and I won't let anyone see that part of me. Stay away or I will attack.* A rageful person is desperate to keep others far enough away so they cannot destroy him.

People are most apt to fly into a rage when they are surprised by a sudden attack on their identity. For example, a friend might offhandedly tell his buddy that his clothes are too cheap and loud for him to get a date with a certain woman. He might be joking, not intending to hurt his friend. But his friend is hurt. "What do you mean, I couldn't get a date with her? I sure look a whole lot better than you do — at least I don't walk with a limp like you." This shamed individual can only think to defend himself by cruelly attacking the other person.

Rage works. It drives people away and so protects the person from revealing his shame. Sometimes it works too well. People start to avoid rageful people who are oversensitive to supposed insults. "I would like to be Mary's friend," the person might say, "but whenever we start to get close, she finds something to get mad about. Then she attacks me for no reason."

The rageful person's strategy to defend against overwhelming shame is very debilitating to the person's self-esteem. This person will probably feel all the more defective when others become too scared to reach out to her. Rage breaks the connection between people and so increases the shamed person's shame. Chronically rageful people become trapped in a lonely world of their own making.

People might respond with rage occasionally, especially when they are suddenly and unexpectedly embarrassed. But persons with excessive shame may express their anger more often. Their regular bouts of rage cover up deeper shame. Their attacks on others direct attention away from their sense of inadequacy.

Perfectionism

Another defense against shame is *perfectionism*. The perfection-ist dreads making mistakes, because she thinks mistakes prove something is fundamentally wrong with her as a person. If she fails at something, she believes she is a *total* failure.

The perfectionist who is defending against shame seems only to recognize two states of being: shameful or perfect. This person fights desperately against being human because he equates accepting humanness with being a failure. But we are all sim-ply human — people who must do the best we can given our limitations in strength, intelligence, creativity, and wisdom. It is not shameful to be less than perfect when none of us has a choice in this matter.

The perfectionist may not be particularly arrogant. She is not really trying to play God when she tries to be faultless. She is simply trying to hold shame at bay a little longer. She feels a tremendous pressure to perform, to demonstrate to the world and to herself that she is adequate. Constantly aware of the possibility of shame, she is convinced that others are watch-ing for imperfections, and when they see her flaws, they will judge her to be worthless.

As you can see, the perfectionist is in a no-win situation. No matter how competent he is, regardless of how well he per-forms, despite all his successes, the perfectionist never feels more than one step ahead of shame. He can delay humilia-tion for a while, perhaps by working harder or longer than anyone else. But he cannot feel comfortable for very long, be-cause he does not know how to accept himself as a good, but limited, human being.

Ordinarily, shamed persons believe they are smaller or lower than others. The words *beneath contempt* describe how shame feels. But what if a shame-based individual could convince her-self that the opposite was true — that she really stood head and shoulders above everybody else? She would have discov-ered arrogance, yet another survival strategy against shame.

Arrogance

This can be two things: grandiosity or contempt. *Grandiosity* is when a person inflates his sense of self-worth so that he believes he is better than others. *Contempt* is when a person puts down someone else to make that person seem smaller than herself.

Here is a way to visualize the difference between grandiosity and contempt. Imagine two people as two equally inflated balloons. Now imagine pumping up one of the balloons until it is so full of hot air that it is ready to burst. That is grandiosity. The grandiose person hides her shame from herself and others by filling up with pretentiousness and false pride. She needs to feel superior to cover up her basic sense of shame. She deludes herself into thinking that she is naturally the best of all living creatures.

Now imagine deflating the other balloon. That is contempt. The contemptuous individual will find a way to deflate other people, making them feel weak, incompetent, and shameful. This person defends against shame by giving it away to someone else. He feels better about himself only when he reduces others to nothing.

Some shame-based persons practice grandiosity; others practice contempt. Many use both forms of arrogance to protect themselves against their inner sense of shame. An arrogant person places himself on a pedestal where nobody can see his shame, not even himself. The price he pays is not being connected to others. Someone on a pedestal cannot be warmed by the beauty of intimacy with others. The arrogant person has set himself apart from all those who would or could love him. True, he avoids feeling worse than others by exchanging feelings of inferiority for feelings of superiority. But he has failed to touch the center of his pain — his shame.

Exhibitionism

The last survival stragegy is *exhibitionism*. This seems to be a paradox because the person who is shamed, instead of hiding, calls attention to herself. *Go ahead, look at me if you want,* the exhibitionist seems to say. *I've got nothing to hide.* This person may act outrageously, flaunting her sexuality, attire, or behavior.

The exhibitionist displays what he would really like to hide. For example, many persons who were victims of sexual abuse as children suffer deep shame as adults. Some of them, however, discover they feel a little more control and a little less pain by wearing extremely seductive clothing or by engaging in numerous sexual encounters. They have survived their early shame experiences by converting their embarrassment and humiliation into public flamboyance.

Exhibitionism is a particularly harmful defense against shame. Every time the exhibitionist goes on display she sets herself further apart from people who are offended or shocked by her behavior. That only increases her shame, which she suppresses by showing off all the more. The exhibitionist eventually becomes isolated, alone, the object of scorn or pity, and, once again, ashamed.

Serious Problems Frequently Associated With Excessive Shame

We will briefly mention some significant problems that trouble many people who are deeply shamed. No simple solutions exist to any of the complex issues noted in the following section. You can, however, start to help yourself by noticing how excessive shame contributes to these problems.

Shame and the Fear of Abandonment

The fear of abandonment is central in people who are deeply shamed. Abandonment seems quite possible to someone who believes that he is basically worthless and unlovable. Why would anyone stay with him when there are so many better persons in the world? Excessive shame prevents a person from believing that he is good enough to be cherished.

"I Will Be Whatever You Want Me to Be."

Fearing abandonment, people who are shamed may try to please others by becoming whoever others want them to be. Their reasoning is clear: *I'm certain that they would be revolted if they saw the real me. I must please them by being the person they would be proud of. That's the only way they will keep me.*

People spend most of their time reacting to others. Their self-worth depends on the praise and criticism they receive from outside themselves.

Self-Neglect, Self-Abuse, and Self-Sabotage

Ed Ramsey, who writes about the need to reconcile the self, notes that shame is often associated with self-neglect, self-abuse, and self-sabotage. *Self-neglect* occurs when a person who is shamed ignores her own needs by, for example, failing to see a physician despite a severe illness, refusing to eat balanced meals, and neglecting her appearance. Each of these actions demonstrates passive self-hatred.

Self-abuse is a more active result of shame. Here, the person who is deeply shamed seeks out ways to damage himself. Certainly, some shame-connected addictive behaviors are nothing less than slow suicide — the anorexic who starves to death, or the alcoholic who continues to drink despite liver damage. Other examples include calling oneself names and knowingly entering into damaging relationships with shamers.

Self-sabotage is another way to harm oneself. A person sabotages herself when she "forgets" to enroll on time in a program that would enhance her career, or by consciously refusing to take medication as prescribed that would ease her depression. She undermines her chances for success and happiness because she thinks she does not deserve anything positive. Internalized shame demands failure. This person chooses continuing shame over success at least in part because her rage at herself allows no room for competence or achievement.

The Desire to Humiliate Others

Shame is a threat to a person's basic sense of being. The shamed person feels small, weak, vulnerable, and exposed. He may rage against himself because he feels unacceptable. He might also find this self-hatred unendurable. Sometimes, in order to survive, a person who is shamed transfers his hatred on to others, treating them with disdain and contempt, writes John Bradshaw in *Healing The Shame That Binds You*.

Who might a person who is shamed attack and humiliate? Too often, her victims are those she has the most power over — her family. These are the ones she criticizes and never praises, the ones she verbally and sometimes physically assaults, the ones she will not allow any success or happiness. The more she loves them, the more she needs to reduce them to nothing so they cannot do the same to her. She shames to avoid her own shame.

Compulsive/Addictive Behaviors

Shame and addiction are natural partners. The more chronically shamed a person is, the more likely he will be attracted to anything that promises relief from internal pain and emptiness. The answer must lie outside himself in the "magic" of alcohol, other drugs, mystical religious movements, consumer goods, sex, food, work, the latest therapy, fad, et cetera. He is trying to fill the void that has been at least partially created by shame. He simply cannot stand being in pain or feeling empty inside.

We do want to offer one caution. Shame certainly contributes to the development and maintenance of addictions. We believe, however, that is only one aspect of a very complicated process that includes physical craving, genetic predisposition, social expectations, and personality characteristics. It would be tempting to concentrate on one component of the problem, namely shame, but we want to avoid oversimplifying the matter. Shame, alone, does not cause addiction any more than an addiction causes shame. Each contributes to the other. The person who is deeply shamed is a high-risk candidate to become addicted, while the addicted person frequently becomes more and more shamed as the addiction worsens.

Sexual Shame

Shame and sexuality are closely connected. Shame generally diminishes interest and excitement whenever it appears. It often does the same with the sexual drive. The person who feels ashamed will often retreat from a possible sexual interaction in the face of that shame. Occasionally, however, sexually shamed persons may become sexually compulsive in an attempt to reduce their bad feelings about themselves. By contrast, people with positive sexual identities have pride, self-respect, dignity, and honor in their sexual lives.

Children and adults who are or have been the victims of sexual abuse are particularly vulnerable to feelings of sexual shame. We strongly encourage these people to seek help through self-help support groups and professional counselors. Everybody has the right to feel good about their sexuality.

Summary

We have investigated four topics in this chapter: (1) the nature of excessive shame, (2) shame spirals, (3) survival strategies that defend against the relentless bad feelings that accompany chronic shame, and (4) certain problems associated with excessive shame.

We use the term *shame-based person* to describe someone whose life centers around chronic shame. Shame-based individuals who are aware of their shame believe they are much worse than others. They see themselves as fundamentally defective, deeply flawed, practically worthless, and less than fully human. These persons are trapped in unhealthy shame.

They are particularly vulnerable to becoming isolated in shame spirals that disconnect them from other people.

Deeply shamed persons often develop defensive strategies to sidestep shame. Six of these defenses are denial, withdrawal, rage, perfectionism, arrogance, and exhibitionism. When these defenses work, the shamed individual convinces herself that she has nothing to feel ashamed of. She will, however, find herself cut off both from reality and from human intimacy. Shame that is avoided remains within, eating away at self-worth. To heal this shame, the person who is shame-based will need the courage to drop her defenses so she can face her shame directly.

Several problems are associated with excessive shame. These include the fear of abandonment and a sense of nothingness; overconformity; self-neglect, self-abuse, and self-sabotage; a pattern of humiliating others; compulsive and addictive behaviors; and sexual shame.

EXERCISES

Exercise One

A person who is shame-based often experiences life in negative ways. He becomes self-conscious, tense, and afraid about his position in the world. Following are statements persons suffering from chronic shame often make. Notice which ones identify common experiences for you.

- I often worry about how I look.
- I am very concerned about what other people think of me.
- When I talk about what I really think, I'm usually embarrassed later.
- I feel self-conscious when I'm with others.
- I have trouble handling criticism.
- I'm afraid I'll be humiliated in front of other people.
- I expect other people to see my flaws.
- I notice my own flaws and faults daily.

- When other people praise me, it's hard for me to believe what they're saying.
- I don't think I'm as good as other people I know.
- I feel shame about the way other people in my family act.
- Sometimes I feel ashamed and I don't even know why.
- I worry about what I'll do wrong.
- I hate being evaluated, even though I know I have done a good job.
- I feel shame just being near somebody who's acting dumb.

Exercise Two

A *chameleon* is a lizard whose skin changes color to match its environment. If it is sitting in the sand, its skin turns a sandy color; if it is on a dark grey rock, its skin turns dark grey. Many of us are like the chameleon, changing ourselves to fit invisibly into our changing environment. Afraid to be different, we become like the person we happen to be around at the time, losing a sense of who we really are. Can you think of a time when you changed your behavior to fit the people around you, so that they wouldn't see you as different? Write it down. What did you gain? What did you give up?

Exercise Three

Many of us are so critical of ourselves that we have trouble accepting a compliment. When someone praises us, we think he is being phony or has poor judgment, because inside we "know" something is wrong with us.

- Do you have trouble accepting praise from others?
- What do you say in your head when somebody gives you a compliment?
- What do you say out loud? Do you accept, reject, or discount the compliment or the person giving it?

Exercise Four

When we struggle with extra shame, we often develop defenses that save us from having to experience it. Note whether you use any of these defenses.

- *Denial.* Joe denies any physical problems, ignoring his back pain because he would feel ashamed to be "weak." *Mary denies that she is anxious enough to need a counselor, because she would feel ashamed to be ''crazy.''* Do you use denial as a defense? How?
- *Withdrawal.* Melody is good at helping others but refuses to accept their help. If someone gets close enough to help her, she is sure the person will see how inadequate she is. *Brian just leaves whenever he starts to feel uncomfortable, never letting anyone know why.* Do you use withdrawal as a defense? How?
- *Rage.* Judy is always telling people off for "putting her down," never stopping to find out what they really meant to say to her. *Alan explodes whenever his children ''shame'' him by not doing what he says immediately — it's easier for Alan to be angry with his kids than to struggle with feelings of inadequacy as a parent.* Do you use rage as a defense? How?
- *Perfectionism.* Jordan dresses flawlessly, with great attention to detail. When a co-worker points out a speck of lint on his blazer, he becomes extremely embarrassed. *Kathy insists that everything in her home be ''just so,'' and she makes everyone in the family meet her standards of perfection.* Do you use perfectionism as a defense? How?
- *Arrogance.* John criticizes his wife for not having interests that are as "socially relevant" as his. When he is not criticizing her, he ignores her, expecting to be waited on because of his importance. *Charlie puts everyone down to make himself feel more important.* Do you use arrogance as a defense? How?
- *Exhibitionism.* Karen wears very low-cut blouses to work every day and "comes on" to all the married men. *Keith boasts endlessly about his sexual conquests.* Do you use exhibitionism as a defense? How?

Exercise Five

In addition to waves and spirals, shame can also occur in repetitive cycles. Here a person does something that produces shame over and over again, such as binge eating or repeating old fights with a partner, never changing their pattern. Circular shame events seem to go on endlessly. Can you think of a shame cycle you are involved in with someone that generates shaming again and again? If so, write on a separate sheet of paper exactly what events occur and in what order.

- List two ways that you could interrupt this cycle by your own action, without shaming the other person.
- Try these alternatives the next time you interact with the other person, and write down whether they were effective or not.
- *Note:* Some shame cycles are so persistent that a counselor may be needed to help alter the pattern. If this is the case for you, and the other person won't go to a counselor with you, go yourself anyway.

Exercise Six

If you are a person who suffers from shame spirals, it is very important for you to learn to think *STOP* when one shame image leads to another. You need to learn to distract yourself by doing something neutral or positive. You must do this *each time another shame image crowds in.* If you find yourself mentally making lists of shaming events that have happened to you, it is important to call a friend, get out for a walk, or do something else that involves movement, contact with others, or both. On a separate sheet of paper, make a list of ten survival options, starting with the one that works best for you. Then, if you begin to spiral down, you can start out by doing survival option one, then two, and so on until you are feeling better.

CHAPTER FOUR

Shame Deficiency

A forty-year-old man has completely taken over a small party. He talks loudly and endlessly about his life, insisting that everyone listen to his stories. When someone tries to change the topic, he ignores them. He insists on staying center stage, as if he thinks the rest of the world exists only to tell him how wonderful he is. He seems completely full of himself and empty of others.

* * * * * * * * * *

A young couple, out on a date, is returning home on a crowded bus. They can't keep their hands off each other. At first, the people sitting near this pair don't say anything. Some of them even smile a bit and remember the times they were deeply in love. But the couple soon go beyond holding hands — they begin explicit sexual activity. Finally, one of the bus riders leans over to another and asks: "What's wrong with those two — have they no shame?"

* * * * * * * * * *

A mimic is hired by a theater manager to liven up the crowd before the main performance. He paints his face and dons an outlandish uniform. He then insults the audience with exaggerated gestures that leave no doubt about his opinion of them. By the end of his performance, he has visually demonstrated just about every bodily function and embarrassed most of the audience. Later, he admits that he would never dare do his act without his mask: "When I put my outfit on, I feel like I get permission to act shamelessly. I couldn't stand it if people could really see me."

* * * * * * * * * *

Having too much shame may be no more severe than having too little shame. People with too little shame are literally "shameless" — they have far less shame than they need to live comfortably in the world. Shame-deficient people may at first seem free from "hang-ups" like modesty, privacy, and prudence. But this apparent freedom is mostly an illusion. Shame-deficient people are not really free at all because they are unable to make good choices about respecting the boundaries of others. They may be ignorant of ordinarily accepted social rules, or perhaps they feel compelled to violate those rules.

The worst problem shame-deficient people have, however, is that they often get so wrapped up in themselves that they cannot connect deeply with others. They have trouble putting themselves in the shoes of others, because they can only see the world from their own perspective. Someone who does feel shame may feel isolated and alone, but this person can use that shame to change his behavior to regain the sense of belonging. People who are shame-deficient don't receive the ordinary signals that others are uncomfortable with them, or if they do hear the messages, they dismiss them as unimportant. Either way, their failure to feel shame can condemn them to a life of separation from other people.

The Self-Centered Universe of People Who Are Shame-Deficient

Who of us, in our secret fantasies, has not imagined ourselves to be the most important person in the world? Who wouldn't want to be adored? For that matter, who wouldn't want to be seen as a perfect person, the embodiment of beauty, intelligence, grace, and strength? Why shouldn't we always have a circle of admirers around us whose only job is to remind us that we are wonderful?

Most people learn when they are young that they cannot be the center of the universe. This lesson is not necessarily fun to learn. The two-year-old child who has to be told over and over the birthday party is for his sister may throw many tantrums before reluctantly taking his place as a mere participant. After all, children start life with no sense of boundaries. At first, they may not even realize their bodies are separate from their mothers or caregivers. By the second year of life, though, they recognize that other people exist. They also discover that others have lives of their own and sometimes cannot or will not pay attention to them. No matter how angry they get, no matter how long they scream or wail, they find that even their parents have interests other than them. Most children resolve this crisis by learning that their place in the world is important, but limited. The two-year-old eventually accepts that he has only one birthday party a year.

Although it might feel wonderful to be the center of attention for a while, most of us discover that it also feels good to care about others. We begin to recognize that a world of shared attention is also a world of mutual warmth and comfort. We trade off the need to be the only person in the universe for our contribution to the safety and beauty of the community.

Some people do not want to accept this idea. Perhaps they never learned to gracefully relinquish being the center of attention when they were children. Later in life, they may have only dated people who quietly listened to how important they were. Still later, their co-workers might have complained that these people worked no harder than anybody else but wanted all the credit. The message they tell the world is this: "I am the most important person ever born. You must give me all your love, time, and appreciation."

People who are shame-deficient often believe they deserve special treatment just because they exist. They want to be placed on a pedestal where they can be worshipped and adored. They simply think it is obvious that they are better than anyone else. They are egotistical to the point of having no room to care about others.

Many unflattering names describe this condition: false pride, narcissism, conceit, haughtiness, hubris. All these words can, at various times, describe people who suffer from deficiency of shame. Remember, though, that almost everyone, at least occasionally, gets wrapped up in themselves. Shame deficiency is part of the human condition, not something to condemn. People who are often shame-deficient can learn new ways to relate to others that emphasize greater respect and interest in other people.

How does shame deficiency differ from the arrogance we described in the last chapter? *Arrogance,* as we see it, is a defense against excessive shame. The arrogant individual may appear to be totally self-centered and devoid of shame. This person, however, actually is full of shame. She is deeply concerned about how others evaluate her, and extremely sensitive to criticism or depreciation. The arrogant person covers her shame with a blanket of superiority. Under that blanket, she shivers with the dread of being exposed as a useless and defective charlatan. She might easily become enraged when others get too close to that shame.

Shameless pride is different. These people stand aloof from others. They are more likely to ignore criticism than get angry because they do not respect those who cannot appreciate them. In fact, they seem often to be indifferent to anything but praise. These people are not hiding tremendous shame with their pride.

Immodesty and the Lack of Discretion

Certain behaviors that are personal such as sexual relations, physical functions and subjects, and some kinds of spiritual worship may be perfectly acceptable, but they are private matters. A modest person does not call excessive attention to himself or his private matters. A modest person seems to have an inner dignity. He does not need to boast about himself, nor does he want or need more than his share of attention.

People who are shame-deficient get attention by acting openly in an area that would normally call for privacy and modesty. Who really wants to hear *all* the details about someone's divorce, underwear selection, or therapy discussion? Ordinarily, shame would tell someone that she has approached a topic that embarrasses others and is probably better kept private. People who are shame-deficient often fail to receive these signals, much to the discomfort of those around them.

Just talking too loud can sometimes invoke shame at a gathering, no matter what the actual content of the discussion. The very loud person seems to ignore the preference of others by invading their boundaries. In fact, shameless behavior violates boundaries, while healthy shame helps us maintain and protect the personal boundaries of others. One reason "good" shame is so important is that, without it, we lose the distinct sense of who we are. Shame preserves and defines our identities by calling our attention to ourselves. Carl Schneider, in his sensitive writings about shame, notes that "shame discloses the self to the self." People who are shame-deficient, then, are often people with little self-awareness. That is why they so often appear emotionally shallow.

Why do the people around a shame-deficient individual feel very uncomfortable? One reason is that most people relate to others through the unspoken mutual understanding called *discretion* or *tact*. For example, we normally would not call attention to someone's slightly messy hair, unmatched clothes, or sweaty face. If something is said about these matters, it would probably be said discretely by a spouse, good friend, or close associate. These delicate topics exist right at the boundary between public and private.

More serious issues also fall on the line between the public and private. Should we bring up someone's recent cancer diagnosis? Is it better to discuss or avoid discussing the death of someone's relative? What if the person you are talking with just lost a job? Would it be helpful or harmful to tell the mother whose son has just gone through drug dependency treatment that your daughter had the same problem? These topics are delicate and might be public information, but the situation would call for discretion, so another person would not feel embarrassed, ashamed, or humiliated.

Every one of us has the capacity to shame others. The more intimate two people get, the more vulnerable they become, because each knows what the other wants to keep private. People need to be careful with this potential weapon. But they will know through their own sense of shame that some things are better discussed discreetly or in private.

Shame Deficiency Discourages Mastery

We gave an example in the exercises at the end of Chapter Two about a man who painted his shed in a hurry, took a long look at the product, realized that he felt ashamed of his efforts, and then went back and did the job right. He felt shame because he fell short of his own standards of competent performance. This is shame at its best, an internal sense of defectiveness that a person can correct and replace with healthy pride. People who are shame-deficient seldom experience this feeling.

Most people have at least a few areas in their life where they want to learn, grow, and achieve excellence. One person will spend hours reading about how to grow roses, while somebody else tackles a new computer manual. One person goes through the motions of a job that demands little, but then goes home and pours energy into his hobby of cabinetmaking. His office partner, excited about the new responsibilities she has been given, stays late after work to make plans.

People who are shame-deficient seldom find these interests. This is not because they are certain they will fail (that comes from excessive shame). They simply cannot seem to find enough internal motivation to propel them toward healthy pride. Part of the problem may be lack of a clear sense of self, a center from which they can gradually expand their boundaries. Some may come from families in which personal pride is unimportant or irrelevant; they were never shown how to challenge themselves. Chronic use of mood-altering chemicals — in particular marijuana — also promotes this kind of shame deficiency: the daily user who quits caring about much of anything has developed "Amotivational Syndrome," the technical term for someone who no longer cares about mastery and competence. This, fortunately, is a reversible condition — the person will usually discover that his normal values and ability to respond to the world returns over time when he quits using.

Shame deficiency robs people of the opportunity to know when they are failing themselves. People who cannot feel shame can become trapped in mediocrity and disinterest. Each shame episode presents an opportunity for personal revitalization, but they miss out on this.

Summary

People who are shame-deficient have less shame than they need to interact well with others. They cannot use their shame to help them understand boundaries and relate to the world.

These people display one or more of the following characteristics:

- They constantly demand the center of attention.
- They often act immodestly.
- They lack discretion and tact in their contacts with others.

- They lack dignity and honor.
- They cannot use their shame to become more competent and to eventually feel healthy pride.

People who are shame-deficient are emotionally immature. Something in their development has gone wrong. They are unable to find their proper place in the universe because the only place they know is center stage. They are disconnected without even knowing it. To put it simply, they need more shame in their lives.

EXERCISES

Exercise One

People deficient in shame often lack humility, the understanding that they are no better and no worse than other people. Because they are absorbed in themselves, they lose their curiosity and appreciation for others. If you often act as if you deserve all the attention, stop talking and start listening this week. Ask people several questions about themselves (not about how they feel about you). Write down what you learn about them.

If you are not shame deficient but know someone who is, pay special attention this week to noticing what cues that person misses and what messages she fails to hear. Write those things down.

Exercise Two

People deficient in shame sometimes break polite rules just to flaunt them. For example, a man who imagines himself to be a great gift to women may violate boundaries by telling dirty jokes at inappropriate times, or by behaving suggestively with women at work. He may believe that the rules do not apply to him and that his immodesty will make him even more irresistible. Have you ever found yourself purposely acting in an immodest way?

Did this behavior accomplish what you wanted?
How do you think others felt?

Exercise Three

People deficient in shame lack discretion and tact. For example, Shirley seriously embarrassed her colleague, Bev, by discussing her "itchy" yeast infection in mixed company at a business lunch. Shirley's supervisor was embarrassed too. The result was that both hesitated to go out to lunch with Shirley again. Shirley found herself increasingly on her own without knowing why. Have you ever violated a boundary without being aware of it?

How did you find this out?

If you know a person who lacks discretion, how do you behave with that person? Do you speak up and tell her what the boundaries are?

SECTION TWO

THE MANY SOURCES OF SHAME

Introduction

Where does shame come from? This is an important question because if we could understand the origins of shame, we could also begin to know how to heal the problems caused by too much or too little shame.

In this section of the book, we will dedicate a chapter each to the five sources of shame. All are significant. None can be ignored if we want to fully understand shame. They are (1) the biological roots of shame found in infancy, (2) shame and the family of origin, (3) current shaming relationships, (4) societal pressures that activate shame, and (5) the self-shaming adult.

CHAPTER FIVE

The Roots of Shame

What are the earliest sources of shame? Does a newborn child enter the world genetically predisposed toward shame, or does shame begin with the first interactions between the infant and his parents?

We shall examine two theories about how shame develops.

1. Children have a biologically given predisposition toward shame.

This shows initially as the infant minimizes uncomfortable stimulation by looking away or losing energy. Researchers of this idea view shame as a universal emotion, with its roots in the human condition, not in specific events involving an infant and his family. Research on depression provides more evidence for the genetic and biological sources of shame. As we shall see, some kinds of depression seem especially related to shame.

2. Shame develops from verbal and nonverbal communications during the first two years of life.

Many theorists and clinicians trace the development of shame to verbal and nonverbal communication within the first two years of life. The emphasis of this theory is on the frustrations that lead to shame as a child struggles to achieve independence and positive attention from parents.

Both of these theories are valuable. We believe that children are born with different capacities toward shame, with some infants probably much more sensitive than others to those feelings. Then parents and caretakers influence the child by either shaming or appreciating her.

No real proof exists for the material we are presenting next. Nobody knows yet exactly how shame develops in infants, and babies certainly can't tell us much about it themselves.

Shame: A Universal Emotion

Research in the area of nonverbal communication has accumulated quickly in the last decade or so. Especially helpful to scientists has been the use of video equipment to study the signals people send each other with their faces and bodies.

A major contribution to this research has been made by Paul Ekman and his associates. In his book, *The Face of Man*, Ekman decided to learn if any emotions could be understood universally. For example, would a native of New Guinea, just by looking at a picture, recognize that a French citizen was angry? He discovered that many feelings do have universal features. Citizens of "advanced" and "primitive" areas alike recognized each other's emotions with great accuracy simply by seeing pictures of each other.

Ekman studied six emotions in detail: happiness, surprise, sadness, disgust, anger, and fear. He speculated that shame and embarrassment could also be universal experiences, noting that "we encountered its expression often enough...to feel confident that its manifestations are also similar across many cultures. One common sign of embarrassment is to turn away and cover the face with the hands."

Another researcher, C. E. Izard, studied feelings of shame and humiliation. In the book, *Face of Emotion*, Izard states that people in most cultures could select the emotion shame/humiliation correctly from a group of photographs showing many emotions.

Silvan Tomkins, however, has made the strongest case for

shame being a universal experience. He has been writing since the 1960s on how emotions are shown primarily in the face. Tomkins, in the chapter he wrote for the book titled, *The Many Faces of Shame*, states that shame diminishes interest and excitement. The person who hangs his head and lowers his eyes experiences less excitation. This need to dampen enthusiasm occurs in situations where too much pleasure would be socially unacceptable or would make a person feel too vulnerable, Tomkins writes.

Shame temporarily disconnects people from each other. For example, women in America and many other societies will often modestly look away when they notice someone showing sexual interest in them, even if they are interested in the other person. The message they may be giving (only under certain circumstances, of course) is that their sexuality is too powerful to express openly in public. Similarly, people will ordinarily avoid eye contact when a situation threatens to become too potent.

How soon does a child respond to overstimulation and discomfort by looking down or away? Donald Nathanson, in the chapter he wrote for *The Many Faces of Shame*, cites studies that document this by the time an infant is eight months old. He believes that infants are born with innate bodily mechanisms that prepare that child for what she will later learn to call shame. Nathanson notes that the more we study infants, the more we realize that we begin to interact with others at birth. If a child can connect with his mother or father from birth, then it is likely he can disconnect as well.

Many parents remember the first time they looked into their newborn infant's eyes. That shared gaze is electrifying — the parent's entire body responds as the physical effects of bonding with that child kick in. That look tells the parents that this child is theirs to love and protect, and it tells the child that she belongs in this world. Eye contact unites two human beings from the moment of birth on.

But the child who looks directly at his parents also looks away from time to time. These moments may be distressing to the parents. "I wish our baby would look at me as often as he looks at his mother," a frustrated father might say. Later in life, either parent might tell the child: "Look at me when I talk to you. I hate it when you stare at the floor." We believe that even a newborn child instinctively realizes that he can "lower the heat" in overly stimulating situations by breaking eye contact.

Shame and Biochemical Depression

If babies are born with the ability to feel shame, then we must consider another important question. Is it possible that certain individuals are born with (or later develop) too much sensitivity to shame? In other words, are some people shame-based from birth because of physical characteristics that have nothing to do with the way that they are raised? Can some people be born ashamed? Do they feel deep, unrelenting shame because their brains send them messages that fill them with self-hatred and despair?

Research in this area has turned up no clear answers. But students of biochemically-caused depression have noticed that it is often accompanied by shame. A psychiatrist, Helen Block Lewis, and others have linked shame and depression. Donald Nathanson writes that certain antidepressant medications are effective in treating the shame that accompanies depression.

Guilt feelings have long been connected with depression. Depressed persons seem to blame themselves for everything that goes wrong, whether or not they are actually responsible. Shame-prone persons who become depressed attack their own personality and character. They, too, blame themselves for what goes wrong, insisting the problem lies in their defective personalities. They insist that they are incompetent, inadequate, and useless. They may believe that they have no reason to live since they are no good. Their unrelenting shame may drive them into contemplating suicide, the ultimate response to feelings of worthlessness.

The deeply shameful thoughts and feelings associated with clinical depression cannot be talked away no matter how caring or concerned other people are. The problem is medical. Shame of this nature is not caused by a person's current relationships, family of origin, or even the individual himself. We want to emphasize one point here: *you need to make an appointment with a qualified doctor or psychiatrist if you are burdened with tremendous feelings of shame that refuse to go away, especially if you have otherwise improved your life over the last few years.* You might be suffering from a biochemically-linked depression that can only be treated with medicine. Please see the second exercise at the end of this chapter for a list of the common signs of depression.

Early Childhood Shame

Most writers and therapists have assumed until recently that shame could not exist until a child began to develop a distinct sense of self. Someone can only feel judged by others if he realizes others are separate from him. A child would not fear abandonment unless he knew it were possible to be abandoned.

Erik Erikson believes that shame develops in about the second year of life when the child is struggling to become independent. Ordinarily, a child at that time desperately wants her own way regardless of what her parents want. (This period is often called "The Terrible Twos" as children battle parents on almost everything.) Erikson believes that a child learns through these fights that she is separate, with her own mind and personality.

Shame can grow quickly in this stage. For example, the child's parents might believe it is their job to control the child at all times. They may prevent him from doing anything by himself. This overprotectiveness, although intended as support, will undermine the child's sense of autonomy. He may eventually conclude he is not good enough to stand up for himself. He may decide he is weaker and less competent than others, causing self-doubt. This doubt may not produce the strong feelings of worthlessness that shame does, but its effects can be enormous. The child who doubts his skills often grows to be an adult who questions the value of almost everything he does.

Erikson describes this time as the developmental crisis of "Autonomy" versus "Shame and Doubt." Erikson believes that parents can help a child develop a sense of autonomy (independence) by gradually allowing her increasing responsibility to manage her own affairs. Shame and doubt are caused either by the parents unreasonably resisting the child's autonomy or by a child's demand for more autonomy than parents can safely allow. Power battles between child and parent can cause some shame. In extreme cases, a child can emerge deeply ashamed of herself.

Like Erikson, Heinz Kohut believes that shame begins around age two. Kohut, in *The Search For Self*, writes that a child has a natural desire to show off — what he calls "boundless exhibitionism." The child expects his parents to pay a lot of attention to him just because he exists. He needs attention to grow emotionally.

Children start their lives feeling they are at the center of the universe. They have little understanding of boundaries between them and others. Only gradually do they realize that other people, especially their parents, lead separate lives in different bodies. The child who knows this also recognizes on some level that he could be abandoned by these people. The fear of abandonment is considered by many to be the core of shame. The shamed person feels he will be abandoned because he is not good enough to keep.

The child struggles for reassurance that she will not be abandoned by demanding constant attention. But no parents can always stop whatever they are doing to watch or praise their children. All children will occasionally feel frustrated when they cannot be the center of attention. This is normal. It even helps a child realize she is simply human. She learns slowly that she is important enough to get attention from others some, but not all, of the time.

But the outcome can also be negative. The child who gets too little attention and concludes that he is not worth his parents' time may decide that nobody really cares or is very interested in him. He may decide he must be "nothing."

When a child receives too much parental disapproval, it can devastate her, filling her with shame and driving her away from others. A child who receives disapproval messages too often may decide that there must be something very wrong with her.

Kohut also describes another possible unfortunate outcome of this attention-seeking stage of life. Children may develop strong narcissistic tendencies. These children may continue to expect and demand more attention than they deserve. They are considered spoiled as youngsters and egotistical as adults. Some fail to mature emotionally and become the shame-deficient adults described in Chapter Four. They have never learned the lesson of humility — that they are not better or worse than others.

Summary

Shame seems to be a universal experience. The physical response of looking down to break eye contact occurs around the world. One value of this kind of shame is that it diminishes interest and excitement — it slows down the contact between two persons before one or the other becomes too angry, happy, or involved.

Shame is connected with biochemically-caused depression. This is more evidence that shame is at least partly genetic. Certain people may be born with a tendency to develop unhealthy amounts of shame.

The kind of shame familiar to adults starts to develop by age two. This is when children begin to establish a separate identity. Excessive shame delays or distorts this process. The shamed child does not believe that he has a right to a separate life, or he concludes that he is a weak and flawed person. His failure to achieve a comfortable sense of autonomy leaves him full of excessive shame and doubt. His inability to resolve his need for attention makes him fear and expect abandonment or demand endless attention from others to reassure him of his worthiness.

The beginnings of shame are still quite mysterious. Genetics and biology appear to play a significant role in this process, but exactly how crucial they are is not yet fully determined.

EXERCISES

Exercise One

One of the functions of shame is to lower the "charge" of powerful contact. Try maintaining eye contact for a longer time than you usually do with several other people. Make sure that you do not hold your breath while doing this, but continue to breathe deeply and gently.

- How do you feel during this extra long eye contact?
- Who broke eye contact first in your experiments?

Exercise Two

If you feel stuck in shame, perhaps you have a biochemical depression. Answering the questions in the following checklist can help you determine whether you need outside help.

- Do you frequently have problems going to sleep or staying asleep through the night?
- Have you gained or lost over ten pounds (without being on a diet) in the past two months?
- Do you find yourself crying all the time, or wanting to cry all the time even though the tears won't come?
- Have your physical reactions and activities "slowed down" to where you don't even feel like moving around?

- Have you withdrawn from friends, family, and activities even more than usual?
- Have you lost interest in sex and sexuality?
- Do you feel significantly worse at one regular time of the day (the morning, afternoon, or evening), but feel better at other times of the day?
- Do you regularly have suicidal feelings, images, or impulses?
- Do you feel blue, sad, and lonely as well as worthless, inadequate, or ashamed?
- Do you have trouble concentrating or thinking clearly?

If you answered yes to more than two of these questions, it is important for you to make an appointment with a doctor or a counselor to be assessed for depression. Take your checklist with you if you are having trouble concentrating or remembering things.

Exercise Three

As children, we need to learn two important lessons. One is that we are worth the attention of others just because we are unique human beings. The other is that we cannot have attention all the time, but we have to share it with others. As a child, how did you feel you were treated by your parents? Circle each term that fits your experience.

the center of attention	paid attention to	ignored
adored	approved of	disapproved of
free within proper limits	controlled	uncontrolled
overly protected	protected reasonably	unprotected

Do you think these experiences have affected how you feel about getting attention now? If so, how?

CHAPTER SIX

Growing Up Shameful: Shame and the Family of Origin

Mother is on another one of her rampages. She is mad at everybody but, as usual, she is most angry with her six-year-old son. "I wish you had never been born," she says. "You're always getting into trouble. You never will amount to anything at all. There is just something wrong with you."

* * * * * * * * *

A thirteen-year-old boy brings home his first report card from his seventh grade teachers. His grades are excellent: four A's and one B. His father scans the grades, briefly praising his son's good work. Then the lecture begins. "When I was in school, I never settled for anything less than straight A's," he tells his son. Thirty minutes later, he closes the sermon with these words: "If you want me to be proud of you, son, you will have to do a little better than this."

* * * * * * * * *

Something must be wrong with Dad. He has been lying on the couch for days now, crying off and on, too sad to go to work. This has happened before, but the children can't remember it ever being this bad. Finally, the oldest child, sixteen-year-old Susan, asks her mother to please call a doctor. But Mother refuses to act. "You know we live in such a small town. If I call the doctor, pretty soon the whole town will know. What will people think of us?"

* * * * * * * * * *

"She's such an ugly little brat. I guess I'm not cut out to be a parent. Every time she cries, I shudder. I can't stand feeding her, and I want to throw up when she needs to be changed. I know I'm supposed to spend time with her, but after a few minutes I start to resent her. A couple of times I've lost control and smacked her, and she wasn't even doing anything wrong."

* * * * * * * * * *

Some families specialize in shaming. Dozens or even hundreds of times each day, members of these families say and do things that create and perpetuate shame. We call these families *shame-based families.*

In some families, one or two people are singled out for shame. These persons are the family *scapegoats,* the ones who get blamed for everything. Scapegoats are given the whole family's shame. Meanwhile, other members of the family seem to be able to do anything they want and never get into trouble. Scapegoats often believe they will always be branded as bad, dumb, or worthless. They carry their shame with them into adulthood, expecting always to be judged.

Other families are so swamped with shame that everyone is affected. The parents think of themselves as failures, unable to earn enough money or to provide enough love. The children learn that there is little in these families to be proud of, and they gradually lose their spirit as they go through life. Everyone in these families criticizes the others. The daily routine is full of insults and personality attacks.

Families promote shame through the way the members act with each other. Children who grow up in shaming families often emerge as shame-based adults whose lives center around feelings of low self-worth and defectiveness.

We will discuss in this chapter how shame develops and becomes exaggerated in shame-based families. Since parents are in charge of these families, we will emphasize parental behaviors that cause shame. Before we begin, though, we want to give a few words of caution. First, remember that virtually no parents deliberately set out to ruin the lives of their children. Shaming parents often come from shaming families themselves. They simply may not know a better way to parent, or they may not realize the damage they do with their shaming attacks. Second, no family is immune from occasional shaming episodes. A certain amount of shame is inevitable and perhaps necessary for a family's normal development. Shame-based families, however, cannot or do not control this shaming behavior. Members of these families often seem to attack each other.

One last word of caution to readers of this book who come from shame-based families: It would be easy to feel resentful as you read this material. It might also be tempting to blame your parents for all your problems with shame, even if you have not lived with them for years. Some of the exercises at the end of this chapter might help you with your feelings. Remember that as an adult you must take responsibility for your own shame. It is important to learn how your parents contributed to your shame so you can begin to alleviate it. Shame from the family of origin is painful and damaging, but it does not have to condemn anyone to a miserable life.

Deficiency Messages

Children who feel defective often have been told over and over that something is wrong with them. Eventually they believe these messages — then they repeat them to themselves until they are certain that they are shameful.

Five messages are especially damaging to a child:

1. You are not good.
2. You are not good enough.
3. You don't belong.
4. You are not lovable.
5. You should not exist.

1. You Are Not Good.

This kind of statement attacks a child at the very center of his being. It tells the child that he was born damaged, that he is rotten to the core, that there is something terribly bad about him and it can never be changed. Some examples of these messages are:

- "You have always been. . .(fat, ugly, stupid, crazy, et cetera)."
- "That's just the way you are. . . . You can't change."
- "From the moment you were born I could tell that something was wrong."

When a parent actually believes the statement, a child can do nothing to make a parent think or act otherwise. For example, a parent who believes his child is crazy can always find some evidence to support this. "Did you see how funny Joey looked when you told him we were going to the zoo? What a strange look. I thought something was wrong with him. Normal kids don't do that, do they?"

The child who receives "You are not good" messages may come to believe that she is inherently defective. She may think that her birth was a dreadful mistake and she owes the world an apology. This child becomes spiritually damaged, seeing no reason for her existence.

2. *You Are Not Good Enough.*

This kind of message is more subtle but just as damaging. A child gets the message that her behavior or personality is almost, but not quite, acceptable. She simply must do a little more. The child who cleaned three rooms really could have cleaned four; the one who came in first in the track meet should have broken the record; the child who did all the wash forgot to fold the clothes exactly right. Other children get the message that they are a bit short on brains or beauty, or that they are a little less likable than their brothers or sisters.

No matter what these children do, they cannot gain parental approval. Their parents always seem disappointed in them — but these parents are quick to point out that their children have great potential. If only they tried harder, they certainly could do more.

Children shamed in this way often believe that they will never be able to do enough to win their parents' love or respect. Nevertheless, that does not mean they quit trying. In fact, they may work to exhaustion attempting just once to hear that they are good enough. They may carry this inner desperation into adulthood only to marry mates who repeat the same pattern of nonacceptance and disappointment.

3. *You Don't Belong.*

Recipients of "You don't belong" messages often feel different from the rest of the family. Something about them is unacceptable and sets them apart. Perhaps they are the only ones in the family with red hair, or maybe they are "too smart for their own good." Possibly the mother or father failed to bond with this child at her birth. Whatever the reason, the rest of the family seems closer to each other than to this child.

Children who have gotten this message repeatedly may be very sensitive to nonverbal rejection. They notice someone's small shrug of disinterest or concealed yawn. They may not be able to put what they feel into words, but they sense that they will always be a stranger in their own family. They desperately want to be accepted but have no idea how to make that happen.

4. You Are Not Lovable.

This kind of message also contributes to a child's sense of deficiency. A child depends entirely on being lovable. Nothing else can guarantee that he will be protected, sheltered, and fed. And yet not one of us can earn another person's love. No child can make his parents love him. The child who discovers that a parent does not love him is bound to feel vulnerable. He is also very likely to conclude that something must be wrong with him. After all, other children are loved by their parents.

Unloved children are not necessarily physically abused or neglected. They might be simply tolerated in their families. They seldom if ever are told they are loved. The parents do their duty but never convey the idea that they treasure their children. Children shamed in this fashion may grow up believing they could never be deeply loved by another human being.

Some parents make a habit of threatening to withdraw their love. They say things like, "If you don't do what I say, I won't love you anymore." They may also reject a child nonverbally by turning away suddenly or refusing to speak to the child. These threats and acts are terrifying, especially to the youngster who has no sense of time. To her, a few minutes of silence may feel like forever.

Parents who threaten to withdraw their love use the fear of abandonment to control their children. They may not realize that they are deeply damaging the child's sense of worth in the process. They contribute to a child's excessive shame when they imply that he is only worth loving when he behaves.

5. You Should Not Exist.

Many children may hear this message directly; for example, a parent might say, "I wish you had never been born." Perhaps a woman became pregnant and it led to an unhappy marriage or economic struggle. Possibly a parent resents or even dislikes one child.

Shaming messages can trigger a strong sense of emptiness and nothingness. Thinking *I should not exist* drains the energy, leading a child to despair. The child who accepts this statement will have difficulty finding a reason to live. Then, or later as an adult, he might even consider suicide. Self-destruction reflects hopelessness. But, at the same time, it is an act of loyalty to shaming parents: *Since you tell me I should not exist, I will cease to be.*

Parental Rejection: Abandonment, Betrayal, Neglect, and Disinterest

The fear of rejection is a familiar theme in shame-bound families. Children may be left alone repeatedly, victims of parental disinterest or neglect. They may be ignored and forgotten even when their parents are home. Sometimes parents get so absorbed in their own lives that they have no time or love to give. Neglect is often extreme when parents are distracted by alcoholism, mental illness, or similar highly stressful conditions. Sometimes neglect is deliberate. For example, we have treated several adult clients who, as children, had parents who would not speak to them for weeks or months at a time.

A child experiences betrayal when promises are repeatedly broken. A noncustodial parent who schedules visits but fails to appear betrays his children. So does a parent who frequently promises to take time with the children but never gets around to it.

The rejected child will often believe there is something wrong with her that triggered the rejection. But each rejection mentioned may encourage slightly different feelings and thoughts.

- The neglected child may decide that she is a "nothing," someone with so little value that not even her parents care about her.

- The abandoned child may feel very lonely since he does not belong to anyone.
- The child whose parents are uninterested in her may begin to feel dull and faded in comparison with others.
- The betrayed child may become distrustful, not able to believe that someone else will not eventually reject him.

The common theme is shame — the sense of inner defectiveness that makes rejection inevitable.

No parent can always pay attention to his children. The shaming patterns discussed here will not occur just because parents happen to occasionally forget or ignore their children. The rejections that promote excessive shame are those that are important, traumatic, or repeated.

Physical and Sexual Abuse

Physical and sexual abuse of children by family members can be powerfully shaming events. Victims of these assaults think that they cannot control their own bodies. They may fail to develop a strong sense of who they are because they can't establish boundaries that will be respected between themselves and others.

Victims of physical abuse are treated with contempt when they are punished. They may be told that they are bad or horrible. It is very difficult for that child to fight off those messages while being physically overpowered. Long after her physical wounds have healed, she will still feel ashamed. She may also experience the humiliation of being too weak to avoid a beating.

Victims of sexual abuse frequently feel dirty and disgusting. Shame and sexuality are closely connected, and the person with a healthy sense of shame will normally also have developed a capacity for sexual modesty and discretion. A parent who sexually abuses a child pollutes that child's sexuality. The shame that accompanies sexual abuse can severely damage a person's sexual identity.

Keeping Secrets: Maintaining the Family Image

Shame-based individuals fear exposure. They don't want others to see them too closely because they are afraid their inner "badness" will become obvious. They often seem to wear masks — assuming roles that nobody can see through — to protect their fragile identities. They are too ashamed to reveal their deeper selves.

Shame-based families operate the same way. Their most important concern is reputation. The answer to the question, *What will the neighbors (my mother, her boss, et cetera) think?* is critical, sometimes more important than the need to face reality. It is as if community approval is crucial and community censure is unthinkable. The image of respectability must be maintained.

Parents who control these families maintain pressure on their children to conform to community expectations. Sometimes, this insistence on propriety is a positive force that helps a child learn and appreciate group standards. At other times, when those pressures are too strong and rigid, a child has to sacrifice great chunks of her individuality in the name of fitting in. The child learns that she can avoid shame only through sacrificing her real self.

Shame-based families often keep secrets. Any number of things may be hidden: a relative's senility; Mother's pill dependency; Dad's problems at work; the trouble a son or daughter is in at school or with the law; a family member's pregnancy, depression, or disease. Children in these families are told (either directly or indirectly) they shouldn't talk about any of these things. If they do, they may be punished for bringing shame to the family.

In secret-keeping families, parents control the flow of information, telling each child only enough so they won't say something embarrassing. Certain members may receive more information than others. Children begin to keep their own collection of secrets, since by now they have decided that secret-keeping is necessary for survival.

Keeping a lot of secrets can make a family sick with shame. People who grow up in these families think there must be something wrong with the family. Who can feel proud of a family that is perpetually in hiding?

Summary

Very few people who grow up in shame-based families can grow to adulthood unscathed. Most carry their excessive shame with them. When they marry and have families of their own, they are at risk of becoming shaming parents who continue the legacy of deficiency messages, rejection, and secrecy. Remember, many parents in shame-based families are themselves deeply ashamed.

Can shame-bound families recover? We believe they can. We have seen families replace mutual shame with mutual pride. They have done this by substituting praise and appreciation for criticism and attacks on each other. Adults can heal their wounds whether or not they are still involved with their families. We will see how to heal these wounds in Section Three after we explore the remaining sources of shame.

EXERCISES

Exercise One

Do you believe that you are not good, not good enough, don't belong, aren't lovable, or shouldn't exist? Have you felt this way a long time? If so, you may have been shamed as you were growing up. See if you can identify which messages you received, from whom you received them, and how you received them. Notice the examples given to help you.

Message:	Who From:	How Received:
not being good	Father	getting hit, getting blamed
not being good enough	Mother	impatient looks, lots of criticism
not belonging	Brother	called me names, left me out
not being lovable	Father	never touched or hugged me
should not exist	Sister	said she wished I hadn't been born

Exercise Two

Abuse comes in many forms, including some ways we might think are normal. Shame-based persons often believe they deserve abuse. Take time now to look at what happened in your family of origin.

- What names were put on you and what you did? Are they complimentary or shaming ("sweetheart" vs. "nerd")? What did they mean to you?
- Were you often blamed for problems in the family or punished for other people's feelings and behavior? ("If it weren't for you..." "You make me mad." "He wouldn't have done it if you hadn't egged him on.")
- How often were you punished? Did you always understand what you were being punished for?
- Were you expected to do things perfectly the first time without mistakes — maybe even things that were really hard for a child your age?
- Were you often ignored, left alone, not spoken to, or avoided by other family members?
- Were you physically abused? (If so, you may need to explore this with a professional.) Were you hit, punched, kicked, or shaken by a parent, by an older brother or sister, or other relative? Did this happen often?

- Were you sexually abused? (If so, you may need to explore this with a professional.) Were you touched in private places by other members of the family, made to dress or undress with observers, or sexually made fun of often?
- Did parents expect you to meet their needs (by saying "be quiet," "get me this," "make supper," "listen while I tell you how bad I feel")? At the same time, did parents often refuse to meet your needs (by having "no time," not keeping promises, not comforting you when you were hurt, not feeding you or taking you to the doctor)?
- How did you feel about yourself (in response to the things listed)? About other family members?

Exercise Three
- Did your family have "skeletons" in its closet? Did family members keep a lot of secrets from each other, or was there a rule that nothing that happened at home could be discussed with friends?
- How do you feel about this secret-keeping now?
- Do you still keep secrets out of fear of what others will think?
- What secrets are you carrying now? What do you think would happen if your secrets were discovered?

Exercise Four
- Do you work hard to do everything right but still always see flaws and mistakes in your work?
- Is there another, older family member who is perfectionistic like this?

Exercise Five
- Have you given up doing anything right or ever being appreciated by your family? Does your family shame you now by criticizing you?

Exercise Six
- Do members of your family of origin shame you now? What messages do you hear? What do members of your family of origin do? How do you respond?

CHAPTER SEVEN

Current Shaming Relationships

Almost all the employees like working for one particular manager in a large firm. Her employees know that she will treat them with respect and dignity even when she disagrees with their point of view. In return, they honor her. She is the one supervisor that is never insulted or ridiculed.

* * * * * * * * * *

"I had to get out of that marriage. My husband criticized everything I said or did. Now I'm in a relationship with a man who actually listens to what I say without interrupting or sneering at me. I can feel my pride returning."

* * * * * * * * * *

"Sometimes I wonder if anybody in the whole world cares about me. Yes, I have a lot of people in my life. But they always want me to take care of them. When I have something I need help with or when I need to talk about my feelings, they all seem to vanish. I feel more like a servant than a friend."

* * * * * * * * * *

It only happens when she returns home for visits and holidays. She starts to feel small by the time she opens the door. Then she gets weak and sick to her stomach. She may be thirty-five years old, but she can't stop those old feelings of shame from coming back. "Oh, there you are," says her mother. "Looks like you've put on a few more pounds, dear."

* * * * * * * * *

Shame begins with the infant, develops in the family of origin, and, as we will see in Chapter Eight, is encouraged by an overly shame-focused society. One significant source of shame is relationships.

Few persons are strong enough to hold up to continuing shame attacks by important people in their lives. Who will feel really good when told repeatedly that she is ugly, incompetent, worthless, or stupid? Who can feel healthy pride while listening to messages that she will never be good enough to satisfy her family, friends, or employer? The formula is simple: the more someone is shamed by others, the more shameful she will feel.

People who have grown up with shame often believe all relationships must be shame-centered. Either they must be told repeatedly that something is wrong with them, or they must do that to someone else. Shame-based persons have difficulty imagining that relationships can include mutual respect, dignity, and pride. The more a person has suffered shame, the more he expects it.

We believe that every person is entitled to a life free from excessive shame. Relationships can and must be built around respect for this to happen.

It is easy to have strong feelings when thinking about shaming relationships. Here again, you may react strongly, especially if you are now involved in a shaming relationship. Keep a few thoughts in mind as you read this chapter.

- First, someone who regularly shames you may be unaware that he is doing so (not all shame episodes are deliberate).
- Second, you may be both a victim and a victimizer. This means that persons who are shamed by others often also repeatedly spread shame as well. Try to notice as you read this chapter how you might be both victim and attacker.
- Third, shame-based relationships can be changed. If both parties in a relationship realize there is too much shame, they may be able to alter their behavior. Shame-based relationships can become respectful when everyone involved understands the problem and commits to do something about it.

How to Tell If You Are in a Shame-Based Relationship

A shame-based relationship is one where the people shame each other routinely. Shame is so built into the relationship that it seems normal. A day would feel unusual if shame were left out.

What does a shame-based relationship look like? There are two kinds.

- One is a *one-way shaming relationship* where most of the shaming is done by the more powerful person to a less powerful one.
- The other is a *two-way shaming relationship* where both persons actively shame each other.

Common Features of Shame-Based Relationships

Shamers are overly critical of the person they are shaming. They watch for and are quick to point out mistakes, using each blunder (real or imagined) to prove their "superiority." They know where others are most easily hurt, and they use that information to attack the other person when there is conflict ("Anyone who would behave that way is a slut, so don't tell me what to do!"). They specialize in contempt and disdain for the persons they supposedly love. They attack the independence of their partners by casting doubt on the partner's intelligence, common sense, and sanity. They actively seek to lower the other person by emphasizing shortcomings. In short, shamers diminish the people around them so they can feel better about themselves.

A relationship needs two persons, and shame-based relationships always feature at least one person in the role of shame receiver. These shame receivers may accept criticism and shaming passively, without argument. They may fight it ferociously, even shaming the other person back in all-out warfare. Either way, they remain stuck, unable to leave a bad relationship or to redesign that partnership around pride, dignity, and mutual appreciation. Shame-based relationships center on the unwritten rule that shaming is a necessary part of communication.

Healthy Relationships

On the other hand, healthy relationships are built on mutual respect. Each person appreciates the other. Actually, the word *appreciation* is too weak; it is more appropriate to say that each person *honors* the other. Each recognizes the inner dignity of the other. They pay attention to the goodness they see and help bring out that goodness. Persons who find themselves in positive relationships will generally feel proud of themselves and of the other person.

How do you know if you are in a shame-based relationship? A clear signal is that you will feel generally competent and worthwhile, except in the presence of a certain person. For example, a secretary who types for several bosses might feel fine with all but one of them. The secretary dreads seeing that boss because he only criticizes and demands the impossible. The secretary can never do good enough work to satisfy him — a sure trigger for shame.

Notice that our emphasis is on repetition. Most people shame another occasionally. The real problem occurs when shame is innate in a relationship. Shame-based relationships are those in which a habit of shaming has developed and continues.

The Symptoms of Shame

If we get shamed regularly by another, we will probably develop many of the symptoms of shame. Some symptoms are that

- we have had trouble looking at the shamer,
- we feel very small, weak, exposed, and vulnerable in this person's presence,
- the longer we stay in the relationship, the worse we feel about ourselves, and
- we feel we are too damaged and unlovable to deserve respect. Self-shaming thoughts add to our shame until we feel worthless and less than human.

People in shaming relationships often feel like children, as well as small and weak. This may be because they experienced many of the same shameful feelings as children: "My husband does the same things to me that my parents did — he even calls me the same mean names." Deficiency messages come in many different forms. They may be

- statements such as "You are unlovable" or "You don't belong"
- threats of abandonment and rejection,
- keeping secrets,
- physical and sexual abuse,
- perfectionism,
- overconcern with public image, and
- disgusted looks, sighs, or being ignored.

All help to transform a healthy relationship between two dignified adults into a shame-based relationship that reduces at least one member to the status of a child.

Unfortunately, once we live in one shaming relationship, it

becomes easier to get into others just like it. This means that if we grew up in a shame-based family, we may be "attracted" later in life to persons who repeat the shaming maneuvers of her family. It also means that even people lucky enough to avoid shame as children can become shame-based adults if they find themselves in long-term shaming relationships. At first, these people may only feel shame in the presence of one specific person. But once people start to feel ashamed of themselves, they begin to lose the ability to command respect from others. Many people finally discover that nearly every one of their significant relationships are centered around shame. It's no wonder they feel hopeless.

Power Through Shaming

Relationships often develop in which one member uses the ability to shame the other to increase or maintain control. For example, a man who repeatedly tells his wife that she is so bad in bed that no man could enjoy her, diminishes her belief in her attractiveness. Once she starts to believe him, she is less likely to consider leaving or even standing up to him as an equal. The more this man can shame his wife, the more power he gains in the relationship.

Shaming like this may or may not be done purposely. Certainly not all such messages are deliberately designed to undermine the self-confidence of another person. Nevertheless, the effect of getting shamed regularly is that the shamed person will feel less and less powerful. One-way shaming relationships will keep one member in control of the other.

Shame may travel down the family power chain just like violence. The strongest member of the family shames the next most powerful. That person then shames the next and so on. Dad shames Mom who shames the oldest child, and so forth.

Power and the ability to shame another may go together. The more power people have, the more likely they are to get away with shame attacks on others. What can people say or do when their boss tells them that they are ignoramuses? Unfortunately, some employers believe they have the right to humiliate employees. And shamed people seldom feel strong enough to challenge those in power, since they have lost their sense of inner worthiness.

Shame increases power differences over time. Two people who started out nearly equal will not stay that way if one is allowed to control the shame process. The shamer will gradually gain control of the relationship.

Some shamers use public humiliation to cement their power. Here, the shamer calls attention to another's deficits in front of other people. A woman who stresses her husband's clumsiness or his small paycheck may do so partly out of thoughtlessness or frustration. Frequent public attacks signify more than this — they make it seem like the person doing the shaming is superior. Here, this woman tells her audience that she is better than her husband since she has the right to complain about his deficiencies. She gains power and control unless her husband can directly challenge her accusations.

One-way shaming relationships distort human connections and are very damaging to the shame recipient. Shamers tend to be hurt less since they control the relationship. But they lose in being shamers. They lose deep intimacy with others while remaining aloof and superior. They lose the beauty of relationships based on mutual respect and dignity. The shamer pays a price for power.

The Mutually Shaming Relationship

Shame does not have to travel in one direction only; it is often two-way. In these relationships, each person attacks the other whenever the opportunity arises. Contests even develop where the goal is to see which person can best embarrass or degrade the other. Shame is used as a weapon.

Witnesses to these shame battles may feel horrified as they watch the pair try to destroy each other. The longer the fight goes on, the meaner it gets. The partners in this battle may finally forget about tact and discretion. Instead, in public they air things that ought to be private about the other person. One may score a victory over the other, but trust is destroyed.

Both participants in mutually shaming relationships get badly damaged. Their worst features are exposed as their personalities come under constant attack. Any dignity they have is drowned in an ocean of mutual recriminations.

Sometimes, shaming couples get locked into rigid roles that only increase their shame. One example is "The Drunk and the Bitcher" game in which the more the drunk drinks, the more the bitcher bitches, and the more the bitcher bitches, the more the drunk drinks. Each can eventually despise the other person. Each may believe the other is the shamer, and he or she is the innocent victim. Neither can think of any way to break out of these terribly destructive roles.

The theme of mutually shaming relationships is contempt. The longer people are in the relationship, the less they respect their partners. They may also begin to despise themselves for participating in these daily shame battles. *How can I sink so low? I hate hearing myself calling him those names, and I know I'm hurting him just like he hurts me when he attacks.* If only the shamers could stop lashing out. Unfortunately, she may not quit shaming him because she thinks she needs to defend herself against his shame attacks. The victim of a shame assault may attack the person who shamed him as a defense. Shame begets shame.

Shame can lock two persons into constant conflict. Neither one of them ends the relationship because that would be the final defeat. Their shame battles end in exhaustion, not victory for either side. Truces become harder and harder to arrange because both people feel too vulnerable when they put down their shame weapons. These people might have no relationship at all if they were not shaming each other. Shame itself becomes the cement that binds them together.

Shame in Nonintimate Relationships

Most of the examples in the previous section refer to persons in intimate relationships. Shaming can also be a significant issue in many kinds of nonintimate relationships. One-way shaming relationships are most common when one person has power over another. Typical examples are

- employer/employee,
- parent/child,
- older sibling/younger sibling (even with grown children),
- teacher/student,
- experienced member of an organization/newcomer, and
- some friendships in which one person is clearly in control.

Two-way shaming occurs most frequently in relationships between equally powerful persons such as among

- colleagues at work,
- friends whose relationship turns stormy, and
- antagonistic siblings.

Shame attacks usually hurt, whatever the source. We have talked with many people who try to convince themselves that they should not let themselves be damaged in these situations. "After all," they may say, "it's only work. Sure, my co-worker is always insulting and making fun of me. But I shouldn't let that get to me." We believe that shame must be acknowledged whenever it is encountered. A person must admit if she is indeed hurt when someone deliberately shames her. Few people are so certain of themselves that they are invulnerable to shame attacks. Shame that occurs in nonintimate relationships, especially when it is a regular and repeated feature, cannot be ignored because it can damage a person perhaps as much as shame that occurs in intimate relationships.

Summary

Shame is corrosive. It eats away at a person's dignity, pride, and self-respect. Unfortunately, many people become embroiled in shame-based relationships that feature daily episodes of humiliation. These relationships may be one-sided — only one member shames the other. One-way shame often occurs when one person enjoys a power advantage over the other. Two-way shaming relationships happen when both parties vigorously and regularly shame the other. These persons engage in shaming contests in which the object is to degrade the other more.

Shaming relationships are dehumanizing. *All of us deserve to be treated with respect, no matter what the nature of our association with another person. Others equally deserve our respect.* Any relationship that centers on shame dishonors its participants.

EXERCISES

Exercise One

A shaming relationship is based on repeated and routine behaviors that send the message that there is something wrong with a person. Using the following checklist, evaluate your relationship with a significant other person by underlining each statement that is true.

The person

- says or implies that I am fat, ugly, stupid, bad, incompetent, inadequate, unlovable, or worthless.
- calls me names.
- swears at me.
- ignores me, as if what I do or say is not important.
- criticizes my tastes and choices regularly.
- criticizes quite often what I do and how I do it.
- criticizes me or makes fun of me in front of others.
- tells me I am not as good as other people.

- tells me how I feel is stupid, irrelevant, or unimportant.
- tells me that he or she is superior to me.
- hits, pushes, slaps, kicks, or otherwise physically abuses me.
- often acts disappointed, angry, or disgusted with me.
- tells me that I am weird or crazy.
- refuses to touch me or only touches me for sex or punishment.
- tells me I should die, disappear, get rid of myself, or get lost.

Now look at your own behavior with this person. Shaming relationships are all too often relationships where both people are shamers, but each only looks at what the other person is doing wrong. So reverse the relationship and do the following checklist, again underlining each statement that applies. Be self-aware and honest as you do this.

- I say or imply that this person is fat, ugly, stupid, bad.
- I call the person names.
- I swear at the person.
- I ignore the person as if what he or she does and says is not important.
- I criticize this person's tastes and choices regularly.
- Quite often, I criticize what the person does and how he or she does it.
- I make fun of this person in front of others.
- I tell the person that he or she is not as good as other people.
- I tell this person that how he or she feels is stupid, irrelevant, or unimportant.
- I tell the person that I am superior to him or her.
- I hit, push, slap, kick, or otherwise physically abuse this person.
- I often act disappointed, angry, or disgusted with the person.
- I tell this person that he or she is weird or crazy.
- I refuse to touch the person or only do so for sex or punishment.
- I tell this person that he or she should die, disappear, get rid of him- or herself, or get lost.

Exercise Two

On a separate sheet of paper, do the following tasks:

Judy and Ray have been married two years. Judy comes from a perfectionistic family where she learned that shame keeps people under control. Judy says Ray should help her by doing the dishes, but when he does do them, she shames him for not doing the glasses first, not rinsing the plates in a special way, and not scrubbing the pans "correctly." Each time he does the dishes, she seems to find something wrong in what he does. This same thing happens when he cleans the living room, does the wash, or drives the car.

How do you think Ray feels about himself? How does he feel about Judy? How does Judy feel about herself? How does she feel about Ray?

- List any one-way shaming relationships in which you have been the person shamed.
- List any one-way shaming relationships in which you have been the shamer.
- List any two-way shaming relationships you have been involved in.
- Do you see any pattern in these relationships? Write down what you notice.
- Now list any nonshaming relationships you have been involved in.
- How are the nonshaming relationships different?
- List the main ways you shame others.

CHAPTER EIGHT

Shame in Our Culture

Just looking different wasn't so bad at first. But the staring, name-calling, teasing, and being left out by the other kids was agony. The older he got, the more often he got messages that he — and others like him — weren't very good and certainly weren't wanted. He became resentful and angry, pushing other people away and hating himself inside. He pulled some risky stunts, pushing himself harder and harder to prove he was somebody good enough to be counted as a real person.

* * * * * * * * * *

"When I was a kid, the message from my parents was, *You can do anything you set out to do, so get all the way to the top.'* Then my coach told me finishing second was the same as coming in dead last. Now my co-workers act friendly — but getting the sales is cutthroat competition, and the contest for promotion is even worse. The pressure to stay on top is unimaginable."

* * * * * * * * * *

"I thought the church was supposed to help people. But sometimes all I remember are the endless messages that I was bad and would go to hell. The punishments and humiliations of the religious school I went to convinced me that if so many others thought I'd turn out bad, then I probably was bad. I still have trouble with that. Some days I feel worse than guilty — like I don't really belong on this earth. I feel unclean deep inside myself."

* * * * * * * * * *

As a young waitress working her way through school, she learned she had to put up with a lot of remarks from customers about her body and her sex life. But she graduated from a tough business school with honors and went to work determined to find respect for her decisions and abilities.

Now that she is a supervisor, sometimes she gets respect. But when she has to pull rank and make a tough decision, she knows her employees make resentful jokes about her 'being a bitch.' She wishes they could consider her as just a boss, instead of always as a "woman boss."

* * * * * * * * * *

Sometimes American society promotes shame without intending to. We promote achievement so highly that many people feel like failures even when they are quite successful. Also, although we state a nonshaming belief that all persons are created equal, we tend to dwell on differences as negative qualities that divide people, instead of positive qualities that can make life richer for all of us. Consequently, people and groups who are "different" are sometimes treated as "bad" or "not good enough," rather than as potential contributors to a richly diverse community life.

American media tends to focus on image and appearance. Though we praise individuality, our society pressures each person to conform to more homogenized standards of appearance and behavior. When we don't fully fit those standards, we may discount our value. We may shame ourselves or others for not fitting narrow societal standards of what is appropriate.

Looking clearly at how shame is emphasized and nurtured in our society today may help us to recognize sources of shame within us and in society. By doing so, we can make freer decisions about how we want to function as members of our social community.

Achievement-Orientation and Shame

We contribute to shame as a society when we expect perfection by confusing "being the best I can" with "being the best of all." Americans can be called "competitive individualists" because we have learned that personal success is gained primarily through individual exertion rather than through community effort. The predictable result is that some of us feel a relentless pressure to prove that we are better than others, in order to consider ourselves "good enough."

This is especially damaging when we learn to focus on competing as families, neighbors, friends, lovers, and teammates and then can't relax and freely appreciate the success of others. When all of us are successful, we become part of a successful community growing in pride. But if we see the success of others only through competitive eyes, we will not experience that pride — we may be envious, or we may feel driven to compete even more, or we may directly shame ourselves for not being as good as others. Thus, we fail to continue our own useful efforts.

Here are ways we may be using society's achievement-orientation standards to set ourselves up for shaming experiences:

- having to obtain a certain position even though we are not suited for it;
- keeping a wary eye on our friends' material possessions; or
- battling continually with our partner in an argument, because it is necessary to win.

On the other hand, ways that we can enjoy the people we live near are to relax, be ourselves, and care enough for them. We can be "on their side" as well as on our own side.

The pursuit of excellence and competence can provide rich goals and values to a life that has seemed empty and meaningless. It can even be fun, so long as we remember that is our goal is to be competent, not to be a star whose fame and fortune far exceeds that of others. And it can be respectful as long as we remember that to be competitive does not necessarily justify doing whatever we want to get there. Healthy competition involves self-respect, and respect for the rights and abilities of others.

Conformity and the Focus on Image and Appearance

Most of us want to look good in the eyes of our friends, family, and acquaintances. We may gain approval by dressing and behaving "correctly," or by conforming to the lifestyle of those around us. We may feel shamed when we stand out from the crowd by looking or acting differently — or when a close friend or family member behaves in a way we consider inappropriate or against conventional standards.

Excessive shame grows in a climate in which appearance means everything. Here the threat of immediate disgrace pushes individuals to conform (or to pretend to conform) to public expectations. Once we saw a woman, whose daughter had a temperature of 104 degrees, stop to put her child in her best dress before taking her to the doctor, in order to keep up her image as being a good mother. Some people are terrified that others will see their home in a less-than-perfect state.

Others serve alcoholic beverages because it is expected, even though they dislike drinking themselves. Some people who seem to "have it all together" are really confused and in pain, but refuse to allow anyone to see inside the mask they wear. Perhaps they fear being ashamed if anyone finds out they are not perfect as society expects them to be. Other people are happy with themselves, but wish they could hide family members who don't fit the proper image.

Excessive shame also grows in a world where an appropriate sense of privacy is being lost. Newscasts regularly feature stories on people in great emotional pain; a grieving person's feelings are displayed for all to view. There is a clear danger that our more private acts will suddenly be exposed to scrutiny. Shame is bound to accompany this danger.

Many of us, wanting to be accepted, may overconform to society's demands. We learn to smile when we are expected to smile, tell others we feel fine instead of asking for help, carefully act like everyone else, and sometimes even begin to think like everyone else! We concentrate on maintaining our images to avoid the threat of humiliation. We may also insist that our friends and family look and act just like everybody else, instead of accepting their eccentricities or allowing them to explore the world of healthy differences as they grow. We become so afraid they will reflect badly on us that we cannot recognize their freedom they need to discover who they really are.

We're not saying conformity is bad. But those of us who concentrate too hard on avoiding any possible shame through lack of conformity may lose touch with ourselves. When we wear a mask too long, we sometimes forget that we can take it off. The danger is that we will forget that people, being human, are unique and sometimes "messy." We may forget that most families have problems and that we can learn to solve our problems and live more happily by trusting and sharing with others. One way to reduce our shame is by sharing our problems in a safe environment. To be always worried about one's image only increases shame.

Prejudice and Discrimination as Shame Promoters

Shame occurs whenever people believe that they are not inherently as good as another. *Societal shame* happens when a group as a whole treats some individuals as less worthy than the majority. Members of groups discriminated against may try to fight off shameful feelings, but many will conclude that they don't or can't completely belong.

Prejudice and discrimination are often supported by societal beliefs that many people see as "right" or "logical," even if they are not true. At times, the poor economic conditions of stigmatized groups may make those beliefs appear to be more accurate than they really are. The boss who fails to hire someone from such a group because "those people are just lazy" may be ensuring that the person looks lazy. If the person discriminated against loses hope, he may fall into despair and depression and lose the motivation he needs to continue to maintain his wholeness and respectability. He may even come to believe that there is something wrong with him and then begins shaming himself.

Many of us fit into groups that are discriminated against to some degree. Some groups that often receive messages that they are defective and inferior compared to others are:

- women,
- old people,
- overweight people,
- alcoholics,
- the physically disabled,
- Blacks,
- Hispanics,
- Arabs,
- Native Americans,
- poor people,
- Jewish people,
- recent immigrants, especially Asians,

- country people,
- adolescents,
- people with Eastern European ancestry,
- people who are bisexual or homosexual.

Certainly, some of these groups face far greater discrimination than others. Nevertheless, shame may be part of the life experience of individuals who belong to any of them.

Societal shaming can come in the form of taunting, teasing, and intimidating. Or it may be more subtle — put-down jokes, continually pointing out of how people fall short, and an assumption that someone from a stigmatized group cannot perform as well as others. The shaming experience can create rage when a person or group is shamed for something that cannot be altered.

We can partly counteract societal shaming by refusing to do it ourselves, and by taking the risk of providing support for those who are being shamed. We can learn to appreciate differences, and let others know that we want to find out who they are, instead of judging them on appearances or preconceived myths. We can speak up against the shaming we see. In addition, we can better understand how we may fit into stigmatized groups, and come to terms with the effect that societal shaming has had on us. We can teach ourselves and our children to recognize, and not be a part of, societal shaming.

Institutional Shaming

Institutions such as the workplace, churches, and schools are responsible for giving order to life. Institutions can be structured to ensure the dignity of people. They can also contribute to a person's shame when, instead of providing strong goals and appropriate boundaries, they are organized in a way that treats the individual with contempt.

The Workplace

A person's work can be a source of profound dignity and pride. But some work organizations treat employees as dispensable objects. Others function as tyrannical, shaming families, or faceless bureaucracies. An executive can be dismissed at sixty so that his firm does not have to pay retirement. A blue collar worker can be displaced, and then be offered the chance to return at half the pay in a nonunion shop. Supervisors can sometimes frighten and harass employees abusively, threatening to take away their jobs if they dare to disagree with them. A heavily entrenched union can demand its workers do less than their best to lower competitive standards.

People who are treated as objects often become deeply embittered; they may begin to feel that their whole lives have been useless. Some take their shame and rage home to their families; others give up. Shame-based work situations can and should be addressed, just like shame-based relationships. Occasionally, people who are continually shamed in their jobs may have to find another work environment for their own mental and emotional health.

The Church

Shame involves a sense of spiritual despair. The deeply shamed person often feels totally alone, isolated from God as well as from people. Organized religion can help heal these wounds by comforting the shamed person and by guiding him back into spiritual communion. Unfortunately, churches may instead add to someone's shame.

Organized religion has at times contributed to the sexual shame of many men and women. When children are told that they are dirty and that all sexual thoughts are sinful, they may, as adults, despise their own bodies. They may not be able to distinguish between healthy and unhealthy sexuality, because they encounter their shame whenever they notice their sexual desires. A person's sexuality can be damaged when she cannot take pride in herself as a whole person.

Many workplaces, schools, and churches are not shaming. But because institutions are so powerful in our lives, setting certain standards for us and structuring much of our time, we need to be aware of the dangers of shaming within them. The healthiest businesses, schools, and churches work to respect those who participate in them, knowing that respecting a person's dignity pays off in increased attendance, loyalty, and work. Perhaps we can find more ways to encourage mutual respect and honor in these settings.

Summary

We have described four aspects of American society that can contribute to a person's shame. They are (1) the unrelenting pressure to succeed, (2) too strong a focus on image and appearance, (3) prejudice and discrimination, and (4) institutional shaming.

We believe that each person can influence society by the choices he makes. We can help society become less shaming in one major way: by regularly and consistently treating each other with respect. We can also learn to understand more clearly that people and things that are different are not necessarily bad. We can take the risk of being who we are.

EXERCISES

Exercise One

The late Green Bay Packers football coach Vince Lombardi said, "Winning is not the most important thing. It is the only thing." This attitude implies that those who are not winners are losers and failures. This type of competitively focused achievement also implies that we must be the best at everything — the best worker, scholar, parent, spouse, child, lover, looker, drinker, athlete, and so on. Just being an ordinary human being who is good at some things and not so good at others is to fail. How does Lombardi's statement apply to you?

Exercise Two

When image and appearance become most important, we learn to mask who we are and how we really feel. Some of us wear one standard mask. Others change masks more often. Find paper and a pack of crayons or Magic Markers. Put two pieces of paper on top of one another on your desk or table. On the top piece of paper, draw a mask that you are wearing now, or wore with someone very recently. When you have completed drawing your mask, take the second piece of paper and draw what it feels like underneath the mask. Don't worry about drawing well — this exercise is just to help you experience yourself differently.

Exercise Three

Here is a list of some groups who are labeled, discriminated against, and ridiculed. Add any additional groups you think of. Check any that you belong to. Circle any that you might have prejudiced opinions about. Be honest.

Women
Blacks
Hispanics
Native Americans
Jews
Homosexuals
Disabled persons
Overweight persons
Divorced persons
Short people
Born-again Christians
Atheists/agnostics
Intellectuals
Protestants

Persons on welfare
Adolescents
Mentally retarded persons
Emotionally disturbed persons
Epileptic persons
People you think are unattractive
Single parents
Abuse victims
Men with long hair
People you think are eccentric
Disfigured persons
People with accents
Catholics
Alcoholics

If you are a member of any of these groups, how has this affected you? Do you feel you have been treated disrespectfully or with discrimination? How? How did you feel about yourself?

Choose one group toward which you have prejudice. Make a resolution to treat these people with respect, equality, and patience until you understand them better. Choose a group with members that you come in contact with, so you can practice this new behavior.

Exercise Four

On a separate sheet of paper, list any experiences of being shamed that have happened to you:

A. The world of education.
   How would you change your education to make it less shaming?
B. The world of work.
   How would you change your work to make it less shaming?
C. The world of religion.
   How would you change your religion to make it less shaming?

CHAPTER NINE

How We Shame Ourselves

She has always felt different. Her speech impediment is so small that hardly anyone notices it, but she can't get it out of her mind. Now she tries to guard everything she says, speaking slowly and carefully when she has to and often saying nothing at all. She is certain that people will laugh at her if she stumbles over a word. She has kept her problem a secret even from her good friends.

* * * * * * * * * *

"I call myself the most terrible names. Sometimes it's because I've made a mistake or said something dumb. Sometimes I haven't done anything bad at all that I can think of. I hear this voice inside screaming at me that I'm the most miserable excuse for a human being that ever walked on earth. The rest is unprintable. I feel loaded down with self-hatred."

* * * * * * * * * *

She is caught in a trap. The worse she feels about herself, the more she stays home. The more she stays home, the worse she feels about herself. She knows this is happening because it has occurred many times in the past. Still, she cannot force herself to call her friends. She is so full of shame that she thinks her friends will push her away.

* * * * * * * * * *

"I feel totally empty — worthless and useless. My life has lost its meaning. I set goals for myself that nobody could meet, and then I despair about my failures. No matter what I do, I can never be good enough to please myself. The funny thing is that I put all this pressure on myself. Nobody else is unhappy with me. Why can't I live with myself when everybody else can?"

* * * * * * * * * *

All people occasionally shame themselves. After all, shame is part of life, and moderate shame can help you grow emotionally. Deeply shamed individuals, however, are so full of shame they regularly attack themselves with this weapon. These persons can truly be called *shame-based* because they respond to the world through their shame. They suffer from such an excess of this feeling that they seem to take their shame with them wherever they go.

The shame-based person expects others to confirm her badness by putting her down with criticism and contempt. Still, the response from others is often irrelevant to the shame-based person. The crucial point is that this person is constantly telling herself that she is no good. She expects others to confirm her shamefulness mainly because she is convinced they will view her in the same way as she sees herself. Nor will this person quickly change her self-perception in the face of praise and acceptance. She will stubbornly cling to the idea that there is something fundamentally wrong with her. She is ashamed to exist.

Self-Shaming as "Automatic" Thinking

The shame-based person has taken his shame into the very center of his being. He assumes, without usually even thinking about it, that he is a shameful person. It is not as if he asks himself each day if he wants to be ashamed. Probably, if he really had a choice, he would prefer to see himself as competent and praiseworthy. The problem is that he does not have that option. His shame comes automatically to him because it is a deeply engrained habit of thinking.

The example at the start of this chapter of the person who constantly calls himself names illustrates this pattern. That person's core of self-hatred and disgust gets activated time after time. He ends up attacking himself mercilessly. Every day he reconvinces himself that he is defective by focusing on his failures and shortcomings. These thoughts appear automatically. They are *thought habits* that do not require conscious decisions. The shame-based person does not have to think about shaming himself any harder than he has to ponder how to tie his shoes or drive the car. He just does it. His shame becomes a type of reflex action, but most of the action takes place in his head.

The phrase "of course..." may be a common aspect of these self-shaming thought habits.

- "Of course I'm stupid."
- "Of course my ideas are worthless."
- "Of course nobody could ever love me."
- "Of course I'm dirty and disgusting."

The shaming thoughts are not challenged when they appear because the person who has them is convinced they are the truth. Her shame is a major part of her identity.

This contributes to the shame-based person's spiritual despair. He cannot see his own goodness when his mind keeps telling him that he is rotten. He will continue to hate himself as long as he continues these thought habits.

Habitual Withdrawal and Isolation

People lose energy when they give themselves these shaming messages. Some give themselves so many of these messages they continually withdraw from others or from healthy activities. They retreat or prepare to withdraw whenever they believe they are once again doing something wrong.

Ellen's story illustrates how a deeply shamed person loses energy for constructive action. A thirty-year-old woman with a long history of alcoholism, Ellen entered an outpatient chemical dependency treatment program and, at first, did quite well. She stayed abstinent from alcohol and worked hard at the program. She felt healthy pride in her progress and began to hope that she could stay straight after she finished treatment. But the thought of success was difficult for Ellen, a woman who, before treatment, had failed in almost everything she attempted. Without much warning, she found her old self-shaming ideas returning.

Ellen, you're no good for anything. Why bother to stay sober when nobody will ever love you? You don't deserve to lead a good life because you're just a lousy person. Why don't you admit that you're hopeless and quit playing games? You might as well get drunk — nobody gives a damn.

These thoughts were so familiar that Ellen didn't bother to fight them. Instead, she accepted them and quit treatment only a few days before she would have completed the program. She eventually used drugs again to confirm to herself that she was a failure. Her habitual shame reasserted itself, causing her to withdraw and isolate herself again.

Imperfectionism

Shamed individuals often have perfectionistic traits even though, deep down, they are imperfectionists. The house must be spotless before company arrives; a project never gets finished because it has several flaws; a person, trying to do a job faultlessly, stays at work or school long after others have gone home. It seems that the shamed person must take great pride in his accomplishments.

Unfortunately, persons with excessive shame do not expect to be competent. They don't believe they are good enough to do well. It is the fear of failure that drives them into relentless action. For instance, the man who spent hundreds of hours constructing a beautiful cabinet keeps it in the basement because he noticed a single blemish and could not accept the idea of human error. That lone defect tells him that the entire project is a lost cause, and that the creator of a flawed product must be damaged himself.

Shame-based people are really imperfectionists because they are continually aware of their defects. They think even trivial mistakes prove their inadequacy. Thus, they avoid activities in which mistakes could be made, or they try to hide their mistakes from others. They may be afraid of being watched, since they believe others are looking for mistakes too.

The shame-based person does not really take pride in her actions. The best she can hope for is a sense of relief: "Whew, I got through another test. Got a B-plus. That teacher must not have much on the ball. He didn't even comment on the spelling mistake I made. I would have given myself an F just for that."

The goal is to avoid humiliation. Nevertheless, she can easily recite her failures, but she may have difficulty remembering her accomplishments. Furthermore, her failures seem permanent to her — no matter what she does they cannot be redeemed. Her successes, however, seem temporary — they could vanish in an instant. Shame is never far away.

Shame and the Core of Self-Hatred

Shame that cannot be removed gradually turns into self-hatred. It is as if there is a "black hole" in the person's soul into which his goodness is lost forever, leaving a residue of disgust and contempt. Thinking only about the badness inside, he misses the beauty of his own humanity. He sees ugliness instead of beauty, shame instead of grace, and weakness instead of strength.

Self-hatred is not subtle or sophisticated. The messages we are referring to are basic and crude. They may include profanity and deprecation. *You're nothing but a piece of shit, or You will never be good for anything.*

Anyone can experience shame and self-hatred. They do not belong only to extremely shamed persons. But most of us can learn to balance our shame with inner messages that we are good and valued human beings.

Summary

We have described five important sources of shame in this section of the book. A person who wants to be fully aware of how shame has affected her will need to consider (1) her biology, (2) family of origin, (3) current relationships, (4) the culture she lives in, and (5) her habits of thinking and acting.

When we look at how we shame ourselves, we can take responsibility for our own behavior without waiting for someone else to change.

We believe that shame does not have to be a permanent condition for anyone. Certainly, some people will have to learn how to appreciate and respect themselves. Those whose shame runs deepest will need to be very patient as they slowly heal the spiritual wound of excessive shame. Recovery is a gradual process that won't always go smoothly. Above all, the shamed person must allow himself the luxury of hope. Hope is an antidote to despair for the self-shaming and self-hating person, and hope is a key to healing.

EXERCISES

Exercise One

Here are thoughts that shamed people commonly tell themselves. Read through them slowly, circling each word that you have used in shaming yourself.

I am defective (damaged, broken, a mistake, flawed).
I am dirty (ugly, unclean, filthy, impure, disgusting).
I am stupid (dumb, silly, crazy, a jerk).
I am incompetent (not good enough, useless, inept, incapable, ineffectual).
I am unlovable (unappreciated, unwanted, uncared for, not worth having).
I deserve to be abandoned (forgotten, unloved, left out).
I am bad (awful, terrible, evil, despicable, horrible, trash).
I am pitiful (contemptible, miserable, insignificant).
I am nothing (empty, worthless, invisible, unnoticed, irrelevant).
I deserve criticism (condemnation, disapproval, destruction).
I feel ashamed (embarrassed, humiliated, mortified, dishonored).
I am weak (small, impotent, puny, feeble).
I should not be alive (exist, take up space).

List three or four messages that you struggle with the most, or that you wish to work on first. Across the page list the new statement you need to learn to make. For example:

Old Statement	New Statement
I am unlovable	I am lovable
I am weak	I am strong

Decide to make one of the new statements to yourself regularly. Write it on your hand. Put it on a piece of paper you carry in your pocket. Pin it to the visor in your car. Tape it to your bathroom mirror. Post it on your refrigerator. Every time you see it, feel it, or remember it, make the new statement to yourself. When you see it and you are alone, say it aloud to yourself. Be persistent and say it as often as you can for at least two weeks. Then write the results on a separate sheet of paper.

Letting Go Of Shame

Exercise Two

The next time you feel like withdrawing in shame, do it — but only for five minutes. Go by the clock, and, after five minutes, *make* yourself move back into contact with other people, either in person or by making a phone call. (If you are in a situation where you cannot do either of these things, write a letter.) Maintain this contact at least ten minutes. Even if contact with others feels difficult, stick to it. Learn to use this technique whenever your shame makes you want to withdraw. When finding someone to stay in touch with at these times, do not choose a person who regularly shames you. Keep trying, even if this process feels uncomfortable at first.

Exercise Three

Shame-based people have a hard time accepting themselves. Sometimes, as children, we find a doll, a stuffed animal, or a pet that accepts us as we are. We feel safer, loving this object or animal, because we know it will not be critical of us or look at our flaws. As adults, we often leave these uncritical, accepting parts of ourselves behind. Go shopping this week and let a doll or stuffed animal "choose you" for a friend. Take it home and let yourself look at it, hold it, even talk to it. Do this in private. Let yourself be a little silly with this stuffed animal, because it will not criticize you. Then write down any ways you recognize it as being like you.

SECTION THREE

HEALING SHAME'S WOUNDS

Introduction

In this section, we will learn how healing the wounds of shame begins with understanding and is followed by action. We will see what actions we can take in healing the wounds caused by the shame from our family of origin, our current relationships, and ourselves.

Finally, we will discuss the help available for the person who is shame-deficient.

CHAPTER TEN

Healing the Wounds of Shame: The Understanding Phase

All her life she has struggled with shame. Now she just wants it to leave her alone. Shame has become her enemy — an unwelcome but frequent visitor that she cannot persuade to leave. Her goal is to eradicate her shame even if that means going numb emotionally.

* * * * * * * * *

"I'm finally learning to appreciate my shame. I used to be terrified of it. Now I can sit quietly with my shame some of the time. I try to listen to what my shame tells me about myself, about how I want to live my life. The most important thing I've recognized is that shame is part of me. If I hate my shame, I'm hating myself."

* * * * * * * * *

This time, he caught himself before much damage was done. He usually makes up an excuse and runs away as soon as he feels any shame. Sometimes he leaves without knowing what is bothering him and only later connects it with shame. But today he noticed right away that he was overreacting to one small put-down.

Then he could remind himself not to flee. He didn't let one small criticism become a total humiliation in his mind.

* * * * * * * * *

If you are in pain from your shame, you can do things that will eventually relieve that discomfort. You can and will, over time, learn how to live in a way that will help you feel competent, worthy, and lovable.

Shame drives down a person's head and eyes. Shame steals energy, optimism, and excitement. Nevertheless, the person whose face flushes with shame is also someone who wants and needs to learn how to hold her head up once again in calm dignity and realistic pride. That is the message of hope that lies hidden in every moment of shame.

The following is meant for everyone, not just shame-based people. Still, we recognize that the most deeply shamed people, those who most desperately long to heal their pain, will read these pages with a great sense of urgency. They may also have been paralyzed so long by their shame that they feel almost hopeless. The powerful despair and pessimism are both part of the shame process and a response to a seemingly impossible situation. We ask that you try to put aside both your pessimism and your desperation for a while. Although we can offer no quick and easy solutions to dissolving your shame in a few days, we do believe there are things you can do to gradually replace excessive shame with positive self-worth.

We have divided this process into two basic stages: understanding (to be covered in this chapter) and action (to be covered in the next chapter). Both are essential to healing shame. Without understanding, action becomes scattered and useless. Without action, understanding fails to help change a person's life. If your goal is to resolve painful shame issues, please allow yourself enough time to both understand and act.

GUIDELINES FOR HEALING
THE WOUNDS OF SHAME

Understanding Phase *(to be discussed in this chapter)*

1. Be patient — shame heals slowly.
2. Become fully aware of your shame.
3. Notice your defenses against shame.
4. Investigate the five sources of your shame (to be discussed shortly).
5. Accept your shame as part of the human condition.

Action Phase *(to be discussed in the next chapter)*

1. Get some help — you don't have to do this alone.
2. Challenge the shame.
3. Set positive goals based on humanity, humility, autonomy, and competence.
4. Take mental and physical action to move toward those goals.
5. Review your progress regularly.

THE UNDERSTANDING PHASE OF SHAME
RESOLUTION

1. Be Patient — Shame Heals Slowly

Shame is about a person's identity as a human being. Since the wounds from shame are frequently deep and long lasting, it will take a while to feel better.

Impatience is a problem as we deal with shame. We naturally want relief from that feeling as quickly as possible. Furthermore, just reading and thinking about shame can temporarily seem to intensify the problem. For example, a woman, when told we were writing a book about shame, said to us: "I hope it's not another one of those dreadful books that only makes you feel worse about yourself!"

Above all, we want our shame to go away so that we can

feel our right to exist in this world. This is perfectly normal.

A real danger is shaming ourselves even more by rushing off too quickly to "fix" our shame. Remember, we cannot force liking or respecting ourselves. Self-caring has to build gradually. Shame can be replaced with dignity and pride, but only slowly. Someone who tries to heal his shame too rapidly may only add another "failure" to his list.

Recovery from shame is a gradual process that can be unpredictable. We might feel terrible one day, better the next, and maybe awful again on the third.

At first, there may be more bad days than good. But after a few months or perhaps a year or longer, you may discover that you respect and appreciate yourself much more than when you first began to heal your shame. The gift of love for yourself is the payoff for dealing with shame and self-hatred.

2. Become Fully Aware of Your Shame

Shame is not easy to face. After all, who wants to study exactly how one holds oneself in contempt? Many people dread the terrible feelings of self-hatred that lie deep inside them and are embarrassed to admit that they have such thoughts. Healing our shame will take courage. We will have to examine our shame even though our natural impulse is to hide from it.

How does someone improve his awareness of shame? One way is by reading books like this and by doing the exercises at the end of each chapter. Another way is to notice the messages our body gives us. Clues that shame is around include blushing, looking down, and a sudden loss of energy — a rapid deflation of the self. We should also listen carefully to our thoughts, especially the automatic insults we give ourselves. We can also detect shame in our actions. If we isolate ourselves from others or withdraw verbally or emotionally, we may be feeling shame. Perhaps we feel paralyzed (the inability to either approach or retreat from a situation because of overwhelming self-consciousness), perfectionistic, or especially critical of people around us.

Still another way to improve our awareness of shame is to investigate our spiritual connections and disconnections. How do we find meaning in our lives? When do we feel empty or meaningless? When do we feel less than fully human?

Shame episodes can be small or great. If we have committed ourselves to becoming fully aware of our shame, we will need to notice the smaller shame events, especially those repeated regularly. Shame can become a habit when smaller shame events go unchallenged.

We may be amazed and discouraged when we realize how often we shame ourselves or how often we are shamed by others. Still, it is far better to learn that we have been living with shame.

3. Notice Your Defenses Against Shame

Earlier, we learned that shamed people often develop survival strategies that lessen their awareness of shame. These defenses minimize immediate pain at the cost of ignoring reality. Think about the common defenses against shame that you may be using.

- *Denial* — denying the parts of life that bring us shame, forcing our real problems out of our consciousness.
- *Withdrawal* — temporarily pulling away from others with loss of interest and energy.
- *Rage* — driving others away so that they cannot see our defects. This is most likely to occur if we believe others are deliberately trying to humiliate us.
- *Perfectionism* — trying to hold off shame by striving to never make a mistake or to do everything perfectly.
- *Arrogance* — acting superior to everybody or insisting that others are full of defects. (Arrogance has two parts: grandiosity and contempt.)
- *Exhibitionism* — making a public display of a behavior we would prefer to hide. For example, if we cannot read well,

we might call special attention to this handicap in a flamboyant way, perhaps to convince ourselves and others that it does not bother us.

We must take time to notice and understand the defenses we use to conceal our shame from ourselves and others. Perhaps one of the six defenses in the list is very familiar. Or we may have developed other strategies that are not on the list.

The goal here is to understand how we protect ourselves from painful shame feelings and thoughts, not just to get rid of our defenses. Eventually, we will be able to make choices about how to live. For example, if we habitually withdraw from others when we start to feel shame (or when we fear that we could start to feel shame), we should not feel obligated to stick around and work through shame issues in public. We have the right to stay or leave, depending on what we can handle at the time. But before we can make any meaningful choices, we must know what survival strategies we are using.

4. Investigate the Five Sources of Your Shame

Shame has many sources: (1) our genetic and biological composition, (2) our families of origin, (3) society's expectations and demands, (4) current relationships, and (5) ourselves. It is valuable to sort through these because each leads to different healing strategies. Certainly, someone whose main problems with shame come from living with an arrogant and demeaning partner is very different from someone whose main concerns are feelings of shame left over from childhood. But many persons will discover that their shame is related to several sources.

Here is an example of how understanding the sources of our shame can be helpful. A man might feel embarrassed and attacked when his wife tells friends he is financially irresponsible. After he has had the time to think about what happened, he might realize her remarks triggered old feelings of shame.

These started when his parents repeatedly told him he was irresponsible and would always fail at what he did. The shame that he must address first is from his family of origin. Later, he can deal with the shame from his current relationship.

5. Accept Your Shame as Part of the Human Condition

The understanding phase of resolving shame ends when we accept ourselves as human beings who occasionally feel ashamed. Our shame won't go away by our fearing, hating, and fighting it. In fact, it could even grow stronger if we fight it. A person who despises her shame forgets that she is detesting herself in the process.

We must accept our shame before we can change it. That is reality. Shame cannot simply be wished away because it is painful. Nor can it be willed away through being tough.

This period of growing self-awareness and acceptance may be short or long; it may take minutes or months. It may apply to your whole life or to a specific event. If, for example, we are suddenly embarrassed or ashamed because of another person's criticism, we can take a few moments to notice and study that feeling before rushing into action. Of course, it will take much longer to fully appreciate the deepest and oldest aspects of our shamed selves. It isn't easy to accept the self-hatred that our shame may have produced.

It is far better to befriend our shame than it is to treat it with dread or hatred. All of us feel ashamed of ourselves occasionally. Try to make peace with that shame if at all possible, because it is really another part of you. We must respect every part of ourselves, including our shame, to discover our love of ourselves.

Summary

The person who is shame-based may have gradually lost interest in himself since he believes he is weak and bad. A person who wants to heal the wounds of shame will have to rekindle his wonder about himself so that he can seek out his lost dignity and competence.

Patience must be blended with renewed interest in oneself. Shame seldom heals quickly; attempting to push it along too rapidly increases the danger of adding to shame instead of lessening it. We can become students of the shame process by carefully noticing how and when we feel shame, recognizing our defenses against shame, and investigating all five sources of that shame.

The final aspect of understanding shame occurs when we accept that shame is an important part of ourselves and that it can contribute to a better life. We can learn to sit quietly with our shame instead of wanting to wrestle it into submission. Curiously, we must treat our shame with respect. Only then will its power over our lives diminish.

One purpose of understanding shame is to prepare us for action. In the next chapter, we will look at healing the wounds of shame through appropriate action.

EXERCISES

Exercise One

Shame heals slowly. What's more, when a person begins to work with shame, the shameful feelings often temporarily intensify, leading her to think she is not getting anywhere. Imagine a person working on shame calling herself a dummy. Then, internally, she says, *Boy, am I stupid for shaming myself when I'm trying not to. I'll never learn.* She has just shamed herself for having shame, and her impatience makes the situation worse. How long does it take to learn to tie a shoe, play the piano, or build a house? It takes a while to regain a sense of wholeness for the self too.

When you find yourself getting impatient, breathe deeply two or three times. Then, while continuing to breathe normally, repeat *I am human* to yourself several times. Remind yourself that — just like tying a shoe — you will learn to deal with your shame, and that you do not need to shame yourself as a motivation. You are okay.

Exercise Two

To become fully aware of our shame, we must examine our defenses. Look carefully now at how you use defenses. Review the defenses you identified in Chapter Three, Exercise Four (page 47-48), and think once again about how you defend yourself against shame.

Here are some examples of shame problems listed by people who courageously confronted their defenses against shame. Use these examples to help you if they are relevant, but do your own thinking here too. Read through these examples and, on a separate sheet of paper, make your own list for each of the defenses.

Denial:

> I deny my mother has a drinking problem, because I would be ashamed to have an alcoholic woman in the family.
> I deny my sexual feelings, because they embarrass me.
> I deny my needs are important, because I would be ashamed to ever be selfish.
> I deny dad abused me, because I think there must have been something wrong with me for him to hit me.
> I deny hitting my wife, because I don't even want to think about it.

Withdrawal:

> I withdraw from conflict, because I am afraid I will be shamed.
> I withdraw from others, because I am afraid what they think of me.
> I withdraw, because I feel different and out of place.
> I withdraw rather than be spontaneous or silly.
> I withdraw and become quiet when I am embarrassed by attention.

127

Rage:

I get mad when my children don't immediately do what I want, because I feel inadequate as a parent.

I get mad at my wife so she doesn't get close enough to embarrass me with her feelings.

I often get mad at other people's stupidity, because I'm afraid they might criticize me.

I get mad at men, because I have been shamed in the past by other men.

I get mad at my dad so that I will never let him humiliate me again.

Perfectionism:

I often don't say anything, because I'm afraid I won't say it right.

I avoid new activities, because I might not do them right.

I make sure everything is in its place, and I am ashamed if anyone sees my car or my house untidy.

I am embarrassed if I find a small flaw in something I have done.

I am afraid the flaws of people around me will reflect on me.

Arrogance:

I get mad at people who think they can tell me what to do, because I'm ashamed to be in their power.

I cover up bad feelings sometimes by acting cocky and superior.

I have to be the best, so I don't have to be afraid of being the worst.

I criticize other people as a way of demonstrating my good points.

I don't have to think about my defects.

Exhibitionism:

I show off a lot, pretending not to be embarrassed by what I do.

I sometimes dress far too seductively or in other ways that attract inappropriate sexual attention.

I act as if I am proud of things I have done when I am really embarrassed about them.

Now — take a minute and relax, breathing deeply. Scan your lists. Do you find yourself using one or two specific defenses, or are you using all of them?

It is all right for you to use defenses — many times you will need them. Give yourself praise for identifying them. If this exercise is very hard for you, find someone who will be direct, honest, and caring with you — and ask that person for help.

Exercise Three

Almost everyone struggles with shame at some time, and many of us have deep shame. When we look at our shame, we often want to run away from it or deny it. Instead, we ask you to choose one or two things that you have identified about shame, and sit quietly with them for a few minutes. Begin to think about these things as simple facts about yourself, just as your address and your height are facts. Remind yourself that no matter how hard it is to believe, there are many other, good people who share these facts of life with you.

It's okay to have shame and it's okay to have defenses. As you work on healing your shame, some of your defenses will become old and unnecessary. You will be able to change them. The facts will change much as they do as a person grows older. Relax. You are okay just the way you are, sitting there this minute. For now, accept being who you are. Just for today.

CHAPTER ELEVEN

Healing the Wounds of Shame: The Action Phase

"All I want to do is to join the human race. Why is that so hard? What can I do to feel that I belong? Every time I am around people, I just want to run away. I'm so afraid of rejection that I stay home all day."

* * * * * * * * *

A man has been having a lot of trouble with compulsive gambling. This time he has used up his family's rent money in one hour of foolish betting. But he refuses to attend any Gamblers Anonymous meetings. After all, he is a successful businessman with a reputation to protect. Besides, he knows that he is too good a man to have to associate with common gamblers. He would not think of lowering himself to their level.

* * * * * * * * *

She yearns to become more independent. But she doesn't know exactly what independence means. Would she have to do everything on her own? Could she ever ask for help? She has spent so much time pleasing others that she is no longer sure about who she is or what she believes in. She feels ashamed every time she depends on others, but she also feels too weak to stand up on her own.

* * * * * * * * *

"I'm tired of failing. I'm tired of expecting that I will mess up anything I touch. How can anyone feel proud when they have a built-in assumption of incompetence? I have got to start taking responsibility to do things well."

* * * * * * * * *

It is not enough simply to understand our shame. Shame is a messenger, telling us that something is wrong in our lives that we must change. We need to pay attention to that message (the understanding phase) and then take action that will help us live a better and more meaningful life.

We have outlined a five-step process to help convert painful shame into positive behaviors. These five steps center around the creation of positive goals, rather than just the elimination of shame.

1. Get help — you don't have to do this alone.
2. Challenge the shame.
3. Set positive goals based on humanity, humility, autonomy, and competence.
4. Take mental and physical action to move toward those goals.
5. Review your progress regularly.

THE ACTION PHASE OF SHAME RESOLUTION

1. Get Help — You Don't Have to Do This Alone

Isolation is a common reaction to feelings of shame. The more deeply a person is shamed, the more she will tend to hide her thoughts, feelings, and actions from others. People who are shamed keep vast areas of their lives a secret because they believe that others would scorn them if others knew who they really were. Unfortunately, shame prospers in secrecy. By concealing her identity, the person who is deeply shamed only convinces herself more that she is fundamentally defective.

Some healing of shame must be done alone. As part of the mending process, we must learn to respect ourselves. We may also need to take time to build or restore our relationship with a spiritual Higher Power to gain a sense of meaning in life. Other people may not be necessary to achieve these tasks, although they may prove helpful.

But, much of shame develops and grows through our relationships with others. That shame can best be addressed when we come out of isolation and communicate with others. In general, *damage from shame begins to heal when that shame is exposed to others in a safe environment.* We need the courage to let others see the parts of us that we ourselves condemn. When we do so, and when the persons who see our shame accept rather than condemn us, we will gradually gain confidence that we are fully human.

Not every person can be trusted with our shame. Above all, a trustworthy person is one who will not add to our shame or humiliation when he is given private information. A good listener here is someone who never shames a shamed person. He is also someone who can share our pain and vulnerability without trying to talk us out of our shame. A good person to share shame with is someone who can also sit quietly with our shame — without fear or disgust.

Because we may have difficulty talking about ourselves, we need to make a commitment to reach out to others at the very times when we feel least acceptable. We need to move toward others even if we are terrified of rejection. At the same time, we need to protect ourselves by seeking nonshaming persons with whom to share, so our acts of courage will not be met with damaging attacks. We may want to begin by taking "small risks," just exposing a part of our shame at a time.

One final note: nobody can respond to us every time with caring and compassion. We should remember this and not expect perfection. We should also not completely reject someone who fails once or twice to respond to our shame.

2. Challenge the Shame

Each source of shame must be challenged a little differently. For example, a depressed woman might need to tell herself all five of the following statements at some time during her recovery from excessive shame.

- *That's my depression telling me I'm no good. I can't stop that from happening now, but I know it's not true.* This challenges the chemically-induced assaults on self-worth that occur during biochemically-caused depression.
- *Women are still considered second rate by many people, but that doesn't mean I have to condemn myself any longer.* This confronts the shame that comes from cultural attitudes.
- *My parents told me I was worthless and I believed them. Now I'm grown up and I can refuse to accept those messages any longer. I think I'll give back that shame because it doesn't belong to me.* This is one way to heal shame from the family of origin.
- *My partner criticizes me ten times a day. It's time for me to tell him clearly that I won't keep living that way. I'm worth more than that.* This may be a necessary statement for the woman to make if she is living with a shaming partner.
- *I'm tired of hating myself. For one thing, I'm going to make a commitment not to call myself terrible names anymore. I need to treat myself with respect.* This challenges self-shaming attitudes and behavior.

Challenging our shame is not the same as attacking it. Remember that the shame we feel is an important part of us. Shame cannot simply be ripped out of our souls and thrown away. A person only increases his shame by attacking it.

We discussed the image of sitting quietly with our shame as part of the healing process. Now we must talk gently but firmly with the shame inside us. The goal is to develop dignity and healthy pride by taking away shame's power over us. We need to refuse to let shame control what we do, how we feel, and what we think. The message that challenges excessive shame will be different for each of us, but its general form is this: *I respect and appreciate the shame inside me, even though it often brings me pain. I know that shame is part of me. But I also am a person who has the right to feel good about myself. I have value as a human being. I deserve to be treated with respect, honor, and dignity by the people around me and by myself. I will no longer live a life centered on my shame.*

Don't expect the shamed part of you to stand up and cheer when you deliver this challenge. Be prepared to spend many hours in animated discussion as your shameful self tries to convince you that you deserve to feel ashamed. The most shamed of us have to renew our commitment to self-worth many times before it feels comfortable. Remember, the goal is not to eradicate your shame, but to return that shame to its rightful place as a "citizen" rather than as "king" or "queen" of your life.

3. Set Positive Goals Based on Humanity, Humility, Autonomy, and Competence

We noted earlier that the times we feel moderate shame help us discover or rediscover important truths about life. Four principles are especially significant in this process: humanity, humility, autonomy, and competence. We might feel damaged in one or more of these areas. We may have even suffered long-term wounds in all four.

The Principle of Humanity

This principle is simple and clear: Everyone belongs to the human race. There are no exceptions. There are no examinations to pass, no duties to accomplish, no possible way to be disqualified. All people are human, and no amount of shame can take that away.

Our goal is to find our way back to the human community. We need to convert the longing to be accepted and loved into positive action. We have to take the responsibility of moving toward others instead of retreating from them. We may have to remind ourselves many times that we have the inherent right to be human.

A person's sense of belonging will increase when he can move toward others who validate and appreciate his humanity. We may want to begin this process of reconciliation slowly. It is fine to start by approaching relatively safe persons or groups (such as self-help communities like Alcoholics Anonymous).

We may need to approach ourselves in the same manner — gradually and patiently. We need to quit condemning ourselves and discover that we are worth loving. We can become our own friend once we accept ourselves as fully human. We may also want to develop, or renew, a relationship with a spiritual Higher Power to reaffirm the meaning of our lives in the overall plan.

We will know that we are living by the principle of humanity when we can say to others we feel close to: "Right now I am having some uncomfortable feelings. Could we talk about them?"

The Principle of Humility

This principle states that all human beings are equal — no person is better or worse than another. If we have difficulties in this area, we usually feel either inferior or superior to others. We are seeing life on a vertical scale where we constantly compete to be better than others, while fearing that we will fail badly. But then we feel contemptible when we are shamed, and we may try to fight that off by being contemptuous of others. This way, life is a shame contest in which everybody is damaged.

We are not saying that all people are alike or that every

action has identical value. Certainly, some persons are blessed with greater physical talents, intelligence, or beauty. But these differences do not make anyone better than anyone else. We can act on this principle by declining invitations to feel inferior or superior to others, and by accepting opportunities that increase equality of spirit in our relationships.

Modesty is part of humility. The modest person has resolved the basic childlike desire of wanting, but fearing, to be at the center of attention. We all deserve to be "stars" some of the time, but not all of the time.

Humility is not the same as humiliation. Humiliation occurs when someone is demeaned and attacked by another; it involves pushing someone into a subhuman state. In contrast, humility is a decision we make to accept our place as an equal to others, neither better nor worse. We can sometimes gain humility by "lowering" ourselves to the level of others. For example, if we have felt smug and superior, we might have to give this up to join the rest of the world. Or we may gain humility by raising ourselves to equality with others by accepting positive attention. The journey in either direction brings us toward full humanity, as we sacrifice being super- or subhuman.

The Principle of Autonomy

Another signal of shame problems is feeling weak and dependent. If we feel this way, we need to set goals that reflect the principle of autonomy: each of us has the right and responsibility to decide how to live our lives. Operating independently means we have an identity of our own. It means we will not have to constantly be "people-pleasers," afraid of being rejected or abandoned. We will have enough self-confidence to believe we can stand alone if we have to.

We do not, however, make independence sacred. We live in a cooperative world in which everyone has important ideas and contributions, so we will strive toward *interdependence* with others by entering mutually respectful relationships.

Autonomy is particularly hard to achieve for those of us who think of ourselves as "victims" in a cruel world. When we are truly autonomous, we will feel moderate and normal shame.

The Principle of Competence

This principle tells us every person is good enough to contribute some value to the world. When we believe in our competence, we'll understand the work we need to do to develop our skills and abilities. We may then feel shame when we have taken our gifts too lightly.

But we do not have to be perfect in anything we do. Occasional failure is an inevitable part of being human. Sometimes, we can learn from failures and go on to become more competent. At other times, we can only accept disappointments, but still we can learn from them.

Shameful feelings can move us toward a commitment to competently perform whatever task is at hand. If our goal is a sense of competence, we will need to change more than our attitude. We will need to examine our behavior to see when and how we act in self-defeating ways. The message we will cultivate is something like this: *I challenge myself to develop the habit of competence. I can replace my shame with realistic pride when I work up to my capacity. But I also know when to stop: My goal is to accept being 'good enough' rather than being perfect.*

4. Take Mental and Physical Action to Move Toward Those Goals

We begin recovering from our shame when we decide we want to live by these principles. We can ask ourselves a very simple but powerful question: how can we change our thoughts and behaviors so we can eventually feel more human, humble, autonomous, and competent?

Here is an exercise to help you to begin this process. First, get at least four separate sheets of paper and label the top of each sheet with a separate principle: humanity, humility, autonomy, and competence. Then, on the left-hand side of the page, write under each heading a list of your thoughts and behaviors that regularly pull you away from these principles. For example, we might notice that we often think of ourselves as failures (violating the principle of competence), or that we almost always ask others to make decisions for us (violating the principle of autonomy).

Make a thorough list, but don't attack yourself. Then ask yourself what you need to do to change each item, and write down those answers next to the original ones. For instance, if we often think of ourselves as a failure, we will want to replace this thought with the idea that we are good enough to succeed. If we go to others for unnecessary help, we can make a commitment not to ask for help until we have really attempted to resolve our issues on our own.

Next, choose no more than one or two things you would like to change. Start with ones that are fairly simple and clear. Finally, commit yourself to making those changes in your daily life, remembering that shame heals slowly and that you don't have to be perfect.

Shame is full of mystery. No simple exercise or plan can possibly cover every part of it. But you can challenge shame effectively by making a long-term commitment to think and feel in ways that consistently move you toward self-respect.

5. Review Your Progress Regularly

Be patient with your shame but don't forget about it. Deeply engrained shame habits are hard to break, and they could sneak back into your life. That is why regular review sessions are helpful. Perhaps you could find another person who is also interested in challenging shame and meet occasionally to review each other's progress. Remember that shame often heals best in the company of others. But even if you have to review your notes by yourself, be sure to do this at least once a month. In this review, you may recognize that you are gradually altering both your habits of thinking and your behavior with others. You may also see from time to time that you are losing ground in one or more areas involving shame. That will be your cue to spend more time thinking about what you need to do and who you can talk with so you can relieve shame.

Your review should be as specific as possible. Ask yourself these questions:

- What have I done in the last few days to help me feel human? Who have I shared both my shame and my good feelings with?
- Have I acted as if I am no better or worse than others recently? Have I started to think of myself as superior or inferior again?
- Am I treating myself as a victim in life? If so, what can I do to return to feeling more in control of my thoughts and actions?
- How am I acting competently or incompetently? Can I now settle for "good enough" or do I have to be perfect?

Questions such as these remind us that shame diminishes when it is replaced with self-care and with respect for others.

Summary

Shame cries out for relief. Fortunately, it points us in certain specific directions. If we take the time and energy to understand our shame, we can act in ways to replace shame with honor and self-respect.

We can heal the wounds of shame in two phases, both with five steps. First comes the understanding phase, which culminates when we learn that shame is inevitable and legitimate. Then comes the action phase, which culminates when we take mental and physical action to meet our goals. These general guidelines apply regardless of the specific sources of shame.

In the next three chapters of the book, we'll focus on healing shame from three specific sources — family of origin, current relationships, and self-shame. Our goal is to help you develop more detailed ideas on how to achieve greater self-worth.

EXERCISES

Exercise One

Damage from shame begins to heal when that shame is exposed to others in a safe environment. This means that we may need to learn to share in a new way, with someone else. It does not mean that we should share with others who shame us, or that we should advertise the things we are ashamed about throughout the neighborhood. But we need to find someone we can begin to talk with more openly. We can start to do this by challenging our defenses.

If you use denial often, admit you are ashamed of something. If you often withdraw from a situation, hang in there ten extra minutes. If you're often rageful, relax your shoulders, arms, hands, and jaw muscles at these times — and stay under control. Then consider *asking* for what you want. If you are a perfectionist, let your image crack — let at least three other people know a way that you are less than perfect. If you are often arrogant, struggle through the nervousness of being an equal in a conversation, or of asking someone else for advice. Try at least one of these experiments this week, and write down the results.

Reread the section in this chapter on challenging your shame (pages 134-135). Practice this technique by writing down situations, and what you could do as an active, challenging response.

Situation:

Challenge:

Situation:

Challenge:

Situation:

Challenge:

Exercise Two

To live by the principle of humanity, we must stop mentally competing with others and looking only at what sets us apart. It is time to look at what we share with other people, instead of feeling inferior, or defending ourselves with superiority or masks. Focus during the next few days on how people are alike by completing the sentences in this exercise. An example of something you might write is, "One way I'm like you is that I care about how others feel. One way you're like me is that you sometimes get nervous."

My Examples:
One way I'm like you is that I:
One way I'm like you is that I:
One way I'm like you is that I:
One way you're like me is that you:
One way you're like me is that you:
One way you're like me is that you:

Exercise Three

We need other people to practice humility with. Shame tells us that people are better or worse than us. Humility tells us they are equal to us. Find someone to explore this idea with. One person should stand on a solidly-constructed chair, with the other person sitting on the floor. Notice how it feels to be way above or way below the other. Talk to each other and notice how your conversation is affected. Now switch roles and talk again. How do you each feel now? Now sit eye-to-eye and talk to each other. Discuss how being "equals" feels.

Exercise Four

To be autonomous, we must have clear and flexible boundaries. We need to know how to say both yes and no appropriately. As shamed people, we often get stuck either people-pleasing and caretaking by saying yes too much, or we get stuck being rigid, dull, or critical by saying no too much. Are you better at saying yes or no? Do you have problems saying yes or no to specific people in your life? Who? Which word do you need to practice saying most? Practice using it three times this week, at least once with someone who is hard to say it to. Say yes or no gently but firmly, and discuss the results with a friend.

Exercise Five

Healthy people recognize the continuum between perfection and imperfection. They know that competent performance is somewhere in between:

Imperfect   Competent   Perfect

Their goal is competence — doing a good job based on realistic personal standards. Shamed people, however, tend to see competence as the same as perfection. Their equation would look like this:

Perfect = Competent
Imperfect = Incompetent

Thus, being competent is either out of their reach, or only possible through perfection. How does this apply to you?

Allow yourself to do three small things competently today, using the healthy definition of the word. Write your reactions on a separate sheet of paper.

Exercise Six

Review your progress regularly by answering the questions listed on page 140 (the questions before the summary in this chapter).

CHAPTER TWELVE

Healing Shame from the Family of Origin

She's only seventeen, but already she's stuck in the past. *Why did my mother desert us when we were kids? What did I do wrong? What was wrong with me? Can I ever trust anyone again?* She cannot let go of the pain of abandonment.

* * * * * * * * *

"My parents kept telling me that I was ugly and clumsy. They told me I wasn't good for anything. But now I'm grown up. I don't need to believe that crap any longer. I can still hear them saying those things to me, but now I refuse to accept it. Just because they gave me a coat of shame doesn't mean I have to keep wearing it."

* * * * * * * * *

His father was a down-in-the-gutter alcoholic. Everybody laughed at the son when he was a child. His ears burned with shame. Funny that his father never seemed to notice and just kept on embarrassing the whole family. Years later, the son still carries the family shame with him wherever he goes. He feels another person's shame, and he needs to give it back.

* * * * * * * * *

"Here's what scares me the most: Yesterday I heard myself shaming my kids in exactly the same way my parents shamed me. For a few minutes I became what I swore I would never be — an impatient, disrespectful, unappreciative parent. I know my folks were terribly shamed themselves. Will this go on forever?"

* * * * * * * * * *

If we were badly shamed in childhood, we might have brought that shame with us into adult life. It is as if we carry around with us a set of parents who live inside our heads. These parent images might repeatedly remind us that we are defective. These "old" parent figures may remain in place even if our parents are no longer around. They may linger even if a parent has changed and no longer shames us. For example, an emotionally disturbed mother or father might have told us we were stupid or pitiful. Later, the parent may have changed and is now respectful to us. Still, the now outdated parent image might stay with us. We need to resolve those shame issues with the "old" parent before we can completely embrace the newer one.

The most common kinds of behavior that produced shame from our families of origin may be:

- messages that we are not good, not good enough, not lovable, or that we do not belong or shouldn't exist;
- threat of abandonment, betrayal, neglect, and disinterest;
- physical and sexual abuse;
- keeping secrets; and
- parental perfectionism.

We strongly believe that you can resolve your shame issues from your family. The task, however, will be difficult because this shame is deeply rooted. Many children absorb the shaming messages they receive. After all, when parents are insisting that something must be wrong with their child, what child can resist these attacks? If this has been true for us, we can examine and challenge our shame in the ways we saw in the last chapter. We will look at more specific approaches that address this source of shame in this chapter. Here are some guidelines.

GUIDELINES FOR RESOLVING SHAME FROM THE FAMILY OF ORIGIN

1. Learn the difference between investigating the past and getting stuck in it.
2. Locate the most important deficiency messages you received from your family.
3. Allow yourself to grieve the losses to your life that resulted from these messages.
4. Challenge the old deficiency messages with new messages that reflect self-worth.
5. Change your behavior so it is consistent with these new and healthier messages.
6. Return "borrowed shame."
7. Consider forgiving those in your family who shamed you, so you can be released from your shame.

1. Learn the Difference Between Investigating the Past And Getting Stuck in It

The goal in studying our past is to discover how events have damaged us, so that we can change our current thoughts, feelings, and actions. While we are "researching" our shame, we will feel pain. But it is important that we work through the hurt rather than get stuck in it. We must bring our heads as well as our hearts with us, maintaining at least some emotional neutrality to balance our suffering.

Try not to exaggerate events as you explore the past. Probably no parent alive always shamed his or her children. See if you can recall some times when your parents or other family members praised you, held you, and clearly appreciated you.

Remember that you are dealing with people, not monsters. Your shame must be kept in perspective to lessen the risk of getting caught up in the past.

The more deeply you have been shamed, the harder it will be to unglue yourself from previous disappointments, traumas, and abandonments. It would be wise to begin this process only when you have developed a support system of people who understand what you need to be doing. These persons may be friends, members of a self-help group, professionals, or family members. You also need to make, and periodically renew, a commitment to the goal of emerging as a healthier and less shamed individual. It doesn't make sense to explore a dark and scary cave without a rope and a flashlight. As you explore the cave of your past, let your friends be your rope, and let your commitment to a healthy present be your flashlight.

2. Locate the Most Important Deficiency Messages You Received from Your Family

The most important deficiency messages are those that affected us most deeply. These statements might feel correct when we say them to ourselves. *Yes, my father always called me a dummy. But he was right. I am stupid.* The messages are painful, and they seem fixed forever. *I guess I will always be a dummy,* we might think. Another cue that we're facing a deficiency message is when we feel small in the presence of the message, as if we are weak and defenseless children. Or we feel defective, ashamed, or humiliated when we hear a message similar to one originally delivered by someone from our family.

One way to learn which shaming statements did the most damage is to review the first half of the first exercise at the end of Chapter Seven (pages 94-95). Then rank the messages based on which one affects you the most today. The top-rated message should be the one that would benefit your life the most if it could be challenged and displaced.

It is helpful if we can remember specific incidents fro
childhood that involved these deficiency messages. Perh
we were called clumsy or lazy by a parent as we did chore
Perhaps a parent would no longer touch us after we reached
puberty. The incidents may be powerful or small, repeated
regularly or occasionally. They may involve verbal or nonverbal interactions. An example of a nonverbal shaming message would be our mother's disappointed shrug of the shoulders or rolling of the eyes in response to our enthusiasm or
accomplishments. A verbal shaming message might be our
father saying, "You aren't good enough," when we brought
home a C or D on our report card.

3. Allow Yourself to Grieve the Losses to Your Life That Resulted from These Messages

Deficiency messages and other shaming behaviors pro-
foundly affect the developing child. Bruce Fischer, author of
the chapter "The Process of Healing Shame" in the book, *The
Treatment of Shame and Guilt in Alcoholism Counseling,* says a child
who receives deficiency messages will have many needs that
will go unmet. These unmet needs must be grieved by the
recovering adult.

Here are a few examples of the losses that can result from
deficiency messages:

- "Not Good" messages promote a lingering sense of badness, weakness, and defectiveness.
- "Not Good Enough" messages suggest that a person will always disappoint others.
- "You Don't Belong" messages generate thoughts of being different from others.
- "You Are Not Lovable" messages predict that a person will be abandoned.
- "You Should Not Exist" messages fill people with emptiness and despair.

to hear that they are loved, that they
good enough just the way they are, and
...ceptable to their family. They need to
...ue human, normal, and competent. These
...eds are not met in habitually shaming families.
...e losses can never be replaced. No amount of praise or
respect in adulthood can compensate for the lack of praise or
respect received as a child. That is why mourning is a necessary
part of healing shame. We must mourn the parts of us that
seemed to die in the face of rejection — for example, the child
who quit believing she could do anything right, or the child
who decided the only way she could be accepted was to take
care of others who she believes were more worthy than herself.

Grieving helps us realize that shame attacks the spirit. When
we face the losses resulting from shame, we feel a penetrating
sorrow that can fill us with pain. But this grief can relieve shame
when it is experienced fully. It helps us to put away the past,
with its lost hopes, so we can find a new path in the future.

According to Elisabeth Kübler-Ross, in her book, *On Death
and Dying,* the final stage in grieving is acceptance. As an adult
dealing with the shame from our family of origin, we may eventually be able to accept that our identity was damaged, and
that some of the losses are permanent. Acceptance of these
ideas allows us to continue forward in the healing process.

4. Challenge the Old Deficiency Messages With New Messages that Reflect Self-Worth

The best thing that can happen to us if we came from a
shame-based family is growing up. No matter how terrible our
situations, we are seldom as helpless and dependent as we
were as children. As adults, we can challenge the bad messages we received as children. We may have had little choice
about accepting these messages before, but we can replace
them now with much healthier ones.

Remember, these messages originated outside of you. They may have been sitting inside your head for years, but they did not begin there. You can sort through the messages you received in childhood and consciously decide to throw some out.

Think of how an infant receives food. Totally dependent on its parents, the infant has little choice but to swallow what it is fed. Powerful shame messages from parental figures had to be swallowed too. As Erving and Miriam Polster point out in their book, *Gestalt Therapy Integrated*, these shame messages were absorbed from the outside and internalized, resulting in our concept of ourselves. These messages seem like they belong to us, but, in truth, we didn't choose them. We now need to reevaluate the role these old messages play in our life.

When we challenge shaming messages from our family of origin, we can take the following steps:

- First, locate and study each specific shaming message.
- Second, identify the person or persons who sent each message.
- Third, challenge the idea that the message must be true because it came from a parent.
- Fourth, consider the message and accept or reject it.
- Fifth, substitute new, positive, nonshaming messages for the old, shaming ones.

For example, as children we perhaps swallowed the message (from parents or others in positions of power and trust) that we were so sad and weak we should be pitied. First, notice how often we now say this to ourselves and how it affects our life. Then try to remember where and when we got that message and, in particular, who sent it to us. Then we can deal with how we began to believe this. *My parents told me I was weak and pitiful. It started when I was sick a lot during childhood. Of course, I believed them, and so I started to act more and more helpless.*

Then, we can decide how true the message really is now. *Now I realize that I can take care of myself. I don't have to believe*

I am incompetent anymore. Finally, you can replace the old, shaming idea with a new self-concept that reflects healthy pride and honor. *I am a competent, capable human being who can do things by myself.*

Some of the oldest shaming messages came to us as infants, before we learned to talk. These kinds of messages result in a feeling of shame that has been stored in the body but seems to have no name. For example, we may cringe and feel small whenever we see a woman pointing her finger at us. This may stem from our mother pointing accusingly at us as infants. This kind of shame sensation is harder to challenge than verbal messages because it was learned so early in life. The same healing, however, may work for this type of shame. An example of challenging this shame would be to alter your body's response to a potentially shaming event; for instance, by holding your head up and responding directly to a woman pointing at you rather than shrinking away.

5. Change Your Behavior So that It Is Consistent With These New and Healthier Messages

The hard work described in the preceding section pays off when you change your actions to live a less shame-focused and more healthy life. This new behavior may begin with acquaintances, friends, and intimate relationships. Eventually, though, you will have to alter your behavior with your family of origin or with others who substitute for your family such as "authority figures."

Shame that originated in your family heals best when you change your interactions with your family. Parents do not have a right to shame their children just because they are parents. As therapists, we hear stories from grown children who still put up with tremendous amounts of verbal and even physical abuse from their parents. We believe parents must earn their children's honor through mutually respectful communication. The first principle, then, in dealing with your family of origin is to insist that you are treated with respect. That means you should stand up to obvious and direct shame attacks. "Dad," you might say, "you have called me an airhead for years. I'm not an airhead and I've never been one. Please don't use that term again."

These confrontations will not be easy. They will probably be met with angry and defensive tactics, especially if the shame attack is intentional.

The best challenges to a shaming family are those that are presented calmly and clearly. They may also have to be repeated regularly, because shame-based families tend to return to old, shaming behaviors out of habit.

Family members can change, and some will do so fairly quickly once they learn that you insist on fair treatment. Others may change reluctantly or not at all. You will have to decide how much time and energy you will devote to the task of changing your family interactions. It is usually a good idea to minimize contact with family members who cannot or will not quit shaming you. Short of completely breaking off communication, you might choose to make shorter visits or phone conversations, or to visit at times or with people in the family where the risk of shame is lessened. ("Now I always take my wife along. They are too polite to attack me in her presence.") Or you can take an active role in setting the agenda for discussion. ("No, Mother, we aren't going to talk again about my divorce. That was over ten years ago.")

If you want to be treated with respect by your family, you should remember that others are watching you for cues. That means you must act toward yourself as you'd want them to behave toward you. It is useless to demand that your parents quit calling you names if they hear you regularly insulting yourself. Nor will others learn how to praise you if you only comment on your faults.

6. Return "Borrowed Shame"

Shame is contagious in shaming families. It can easily pass from one family member to another, finally affecting everyone. Sometimes one or more persons will gather the shame that belonged to another family member. This shame is transferred from its rightful owner to more vulnerable people. The man whose ears burned with shame as a child because of his father's alcoholism is a good example of this.

We call this shame "borrowed" to keep the focus on the possibility of returning it to its original owner. The idea is that, at one time, a person was "loaned" shame against his or her will. This shame originated from the behavior or attitudes of another, usually more powerful, family member. Now, that shame must be returned before the healing person can embrace a nonshaming view of himself. All that is meant by returning borrowed shame is letting others take responsibility for their own behavior or feelings.

Transferred shame may be given to a specific family member either intentionally or unintentionally. Often, it happens when the family cannot stand the humiliation of the real problem. For example, it is far easier to blame and shame a child than to cope with a father's drunkenness. ("You ought to be ashamed of yourself, young man. If you got better grades and caused less grief around here, your father wouldn't get so upset and have to drink.")

Certain children may be blamed the most for family troubles. But others in the family may also "borrow" shame. Other children are held up as examples and will collect shame and guilt when they fail to keep everybody happy and everything "perfect." Parents can and do feel "borrowed shame" as well, for the actions of a child.

The key to healing the wounds received from "borrowed shame" is in recognizing when you are feeling shame about something that has nothing really to do with your actions, but results from another family member's behavior. If you are returning "borrowed shame," you may tell yourself, *Long ago I took on some shame that didn't belong to me. I thought it was mine at the time. So did the rest of my family. But now I know that I did nothing at the time that was wrong. I'm not guilty, and I have nothing to feel ashamed about.*

Here are examples of three people who returned "borrowed shame."

* * * * * * * * * *

Lisa is an incest victim whose father is dead. Lisa gathered a "shame bouquet" of dry grass, thorns, a vine with dead fruit, and small flowers. She took it to her father's grave, and gave her shame back to him — where it had originated — saying the things she needed to, to free herself.

* * * * * * * * * *

Rick's mother was very critical, always shaming him for something because of her own unhappiness. For years he had accepted her evaluation that he was bad. She would not listen to Rick's gentle challenges, and he was afraid of her because she had a terrible temper. When Rick was ready, he went to a hardware store and bought a large shovel. He put a bow on it, and gave it to her as a present. In the future when she shamed him, he would tell himself, *She can shovel her own shit now.* Then he would put on his hat and leave.

* * * * * * * * * *

Paula is one of six children. Her brothers carouse and get in trouble, and she used to blame herself. She would bail them out because of her shame. She returned this borrowed shame by recognizing that her brothers were old enough to take responsibility for their own actions, and that she was not an extension of them. In her own mind, she saw herself as a distinct and special individual. Then she set limits on how she would relate to her brothers and told them the limits tactfully but firmly. Paula is no longer ashamed of herself.

* * * * * * * * * *

Should you directly communicate your resolve to other family members? Yes, if some people in your family can understand what you mean. Yes, if family members still insist on shaming you through transferring their shame. The main goal here, however, is for the shamed individual to return borrowed shame that damages his spirit, not to punish others by insisting that they now should feel humiliated.

7. Consider Forgiving Those in Your Family Who Shamed You, So You Can Be Released from Your Shame

Forgiveness may be quite painful. It may bring strong feelings of rage, hatred, despair, and profound sadness to the surface. These feelings are responses to the unnecessary destruction caused by excessive shaming.

Anger is appropriate during this exploration of our youth. The anger tells us that something wrong happened. It can provide energy for us to make changes in our thoughts and behaviors. We should be careful, however, that our anger doesn't turn into resentment, a far less productive emotion. A resentful person is someone who is holding on to anger and does not want to give it up and go ahead with living.

Forgiveness is a way to release resentments. The purpose of forgiveness is healing ourselves. Forgiveness might lead toward a reconciliation with the person who damaged us or with our memories of that person. Or forgiveness may allow us to end a relationship that has been based on pain and resentment and get on with our life.

Remember, forgiveness is optional. Maybe we feel the wounds we suffered were too great to forgive. Maybe we want to forgive but cannot find the spirit within to do so. Forgiving has meaning only when we realize that we have no obligation to forgive. In other words, forgiveness works best when it is seen as a free gift that we give ourselves with no strings attached. True forgiveness makes no demand. If we forgive another, we do not necessarily have to love her, reconcile with her, or forget about what happened.

Forgiveness is both an attitude and a framework for action. Typically, we will recognize that we have spent too much time bitterly thinking about how badly we were treated. A change in attitude is signaled by thoughts like these: *I am tired of resentments. They keep me angry and stuck in the past. They only add to my shame. I am ready to forgive the people who shamed me so that I can get on with my life.*

This change of heart leads toward new behavior. The energy that had been trapped in resentment is now available for self-caring. You might also find that you can now approach your parents differently. *Holidays used to be horrible. I'd spend the whole time arguing with my parents over little things. Now I can accept what happened in the past; I don't have to find ways to attack them.*

Summary

Shame rooted in the family of origin is painful, tenacious, and damaging. Still, it can be healed. The process involves focusing on the deficiency messages that most harmed us, and grieving the losses that resulted from those messages. Then we can challenge the messages and change our behavior in ways that reflect pride, honor, and dignity rather than shame. We need to return "borrowed" or transferred shame, and consider forgiveness as a way to release ourselves from shame.

The wounds of shame we got from our families of origin heal slowly. We will need to bring into this effort our feelings, thoughts, behaviors, and spirit. Just remember that change is possible. We don't have to live stuck in shame from the past.

EXERCISES

Exercise One

The person who wants to heal from shame must learn which shaming statements did the most damage. Rank the following messages based on their effects on you today from one (strongest) to five (weakest).

Deficiency Messages	My Order of Importance
I'm not good	
I'm not good enough	
I don't belong	
I'm not lovable	
I shouldn't exist	

Starting with message number one, list on a separate sheet of paper how you received this message. List as many incidents as possible. If your family was extremely shaming, focus on messages you received from one person at a time. Do as much as you can here without going into a tailspin. The heading on your sheet of paper should look like this:

Message: *Incidents:*

Be gentle with yourself. If you begin to feel too bad, leave the list for a couple of days. Be patient. The list of specific incidents may only come to you over a period of several days. If you have no memory of your childhood, and this list is impossible to do, go back to accepting and loving a stuffed animal that reminds you of yourself, or perhaps of yourself as a child. The incidents you are asked to think of in this exercise will come to your mind when you are ready to deal with them.

Although this list can seem overwhelming, it is our experience that most people's lists contain what they are indeed ready to work through — no more incidents and no less. Do use your support system as you need it; don't hesitate to get a counselor's help if you or someone in your support system feels that it is important.

Now list what you lost from these incidents. For example, one person's list included respect for oneself, respect for a parent, virginity, the right to say no and still be loved, a sense of belonging, the ability to feel secure, contact with a particular person, and the ability to recognize that he could do something good. Include physical, mental, and emotional injuries on this list, as they are losses of health. The third heading on your sheet of paper should look like this:

What I Lost:

Exercise Two

Focus on one incident, and remember it the best you can. Close your eyes and remember yourself as a child being shamed. What did you see? Hear? Feel? If you have a young friend who had a similar incident happen to them, what would that person need to hear? In your mind's eye (or physically, using a stuffed animal), reach out and hold the child that is you, and tell it what it needed to hear then. Then give yourself the message you need to hear now.

- *I am good.*
- *I am good enough.*
- *I am lovable.*
- *I do belong.*
- *It's good that I exist.*

It is all right to be emotional during this exercise but not necessary. The goal for these few minutes is to be compassionate, comforting, and loving to ourselves, and for us to begin to grieve our losses without having to run from ourselves. (Note: If you seem unable to mentally reach out to the child in your past, relax. Someday you will be able to do this.)

Exercise Three

We need to share our sadness and pain by doing one or more of the following tasks:

- Share it with someone in your support system and ask for comfort.
- Write it in your journal and get it out of your system.
- Share it with a Higher Power and let it heal slowly.
- Share it with the wind and let the wind blow your pain away.

You may be able to think of other ways to do your sharing. Write down the things you have done.

Exercise Four

List at least three ways in which you will begin to give yourself positive messages by changing your behavior to demonstrate clear self-respect.

If these ways include challenging current shaming practices in your family of origin, choose a specific problem to start with. Don't start with the biggest problem — work up to that one. Do the following.

- Who shames me?
- Specific shaming behavior:
- Possible ways to challenge this behavior:

Put a checkmark by the method you will try.
After you have challenged the behavior, answer these questions:

- Was I respectful?
- Did I stay calm?
- Was I clear?
- Was I heard?
- Will I try again or minimize contact? Why?

Exercise Five

"Borrowed shame" is not always easy to return. This, in part, is due to the irrational guilt often connected with it. For instance, we think that our family member would not have behaved so shamefully if there was not something wrong with us. Because of our mistaken belief, we take responsibility for that person's shame or his or her shaming attitudes.

Answer the following questions on a separate sheet of paper:

- How have I "borrowed shame"?
- What do I need to do to return this "borrowed shame"?

Exercise Six

Forgiving those who have shamed us is an important part of the healing process. It means accepting them as they are, just as we are accepting ourselves as we are. It is not an obligation, and it is not an endorsement of their behavior, only of our mutual humanity. Forgiving should be done only as a final step in the healing process, not as a first or second step. Most people must allow themselves to be angry first. Forgiveness shouldn't be used to short-circuit the healthy anger that helps us form a distinct new identity.

When you are sure you are ready to forgive, or if you have built up high resentment and need to practice forgiving for your own health and well-being, return to this exercise and complete it.

Now that you are willing to forgive, begin by naming the person you wish to forgive and listing anything you have gained, learned, or are grateful for in relation to him or her. List only real positives.

Now list the nicest things you can imagine happening to this person, including nice things you wish would happen to you.

Breathe deeply and relax. Imagine one or more of these good things happening to the person you are forgiving. Imagine it happening again. And again. Get as clear a mental image as you can. Each day for five minutes, see good things happening to the person you are forgiving. Do this until you feel really happy as you see this happen. Continue the exercise until every time you think of this person, you feel serene.

If you have an uncomfortable relationship with this person, limit the time you spend with him or her, and take care of your feelings as you go. You are forgiving this person in order to improve your own well-being — regardless of whether the person benefits from your change of attitude. Do not expect the person to change in response to your forgiveness — forgiveness is a gift with no strings attached.

CHAPTER THIRTEEN

Healing Shame in Current Relationships

They are an amazing couple. He tells her she is a lousy mother, while she faults his ability to show feelings. They go on and on like that. Then they feel awful about what has happened to them — how hate and shame have replaced love and honor. They need to call a truce, but each person is afraid to stop attacking the other.

* * * * * * * * *

"For years I took his inventory. I watched his every movement for signs that he wanted to put me down. I never even noticed how I shamed him. If I did, I justified my behavior by telling myself I was only defending myself. Things didn't start to change until I made some commitments to quit shaming him."

* * * * * * * * *

"Enough is enough. I've explained to my partner that I will no longer tolerate his abuse. But he refuses to change. Every day he still calls me names in front of our friends. He says I deserve it, and he won't accept any responsibility for his actions. I can't live with him much longer. How can I feel less shame when he deliberately adds to my shame?"

* * * * * * * * *

The issue is power. She uses her ability to shame others like a club. Colleagues at work, friends, and family all fear her sudden attacks. She can make people feel small just by looking at them. Shame — the way she keeps others under control — is her best weapon.

* * * * * * * * *

Shame-based relationships are those that center around excessive shame. This shame may flow in one direction only (usually from a more powerful person toward a weaker person), or it might flow in both directions through mutually destructive shame contests. Either way, relationships built around shame damage the participants, even those who seem to gain power and control. Shame-based relationships damage the dignity of everybody and minimize the possibility for deeper intimacy.

The goal, then, is to exchange or alter shame-based relationships to relationships that center around honor, respect, and dignity. Here are some guidelines designed to help you reach that goal.

GUIDELINES FOR HEALING SHAME-BASED CURRENT RELATIONSHIPS

1. Begin by becoming aware of how you shame others in your important relationships.
2. Notice what you gain through shaming others.
3. Notice what damage occurs to yourself and others through your shaming behavior.

4. Connect your shaming behavior with your own shame and self-hatred issues.
5. Make a commitment to quit shaming others, regardless of their behavior toward you.
6. Replace shaming behavior with respectful actions toward others.
7. Notice how you are shamed by significant others and the damage done.
8. Confront and challenge shaming behavior that is directed toward you.
9. Consider leaving relationships that remain shame-based.
10. Make and keep a commitment to nurture nonshaming relationships.

1. Begin by Becoming Aware of How You Shame Others In Your Important Relationships

Frankly, it is much easier for most people to pay attention to how others shame them than to look at their own shaming actions. We suggest that it is more productive to begin by looking at our tendency to shame the important persons in our lives. This is particularly true for two-way shaming relationships in which both parties use shame as a weapon to gain power and control.

Here is a typical example: A couple complains that all they do is bicker and fight. Then each spends hours pointing out exactly what the other does that distresses him or her. Neither partner has much interest in listening to the other; they are too busy attacking. Each is well aware of how he or she is being shamed, but both are unwilling to change their shaming behavior.

Nobody gives up power easily. That general principle leads to a more specific one: nobody gives up the power of shaming others easily. So, before asking someone to stop shaming you, it's vital that you honestly evaluate your own words, thoughts, and actions.

Start by recognizing the most direct and forceful shame attacks. These are deliberate insults you heap on your partner (or other important people in your life). Some of these insults might be spoken in public — a good name for these is *humiliations*. Others will be more private, but they are perhaps equally damaging. These insults are usually predictable in a long-term relationship. They are open signs of contempt for the other person. When they work, they diminish and weaken your partner.

Then think about the more subtle ways that you demean others. Do you roll your eyes in disgust when your children try to talk with you? Do you interrupt your partner regularly because you think you know so much more? Do you chuckle a little too often at his serious remarks? Are you so bored with someone's remarks that you don't even listen when she speaks? How else do you subtly shame the people around you?

What if you can find no evidence that you shame another person? First, go back and look again. Remember that it is hard to face this part of ourselves, and so it is easy to deny shaming behavior. Next, check with others directly, by asking them if and when they feel shamed by you, and by noticing their reactions to your behavior. Watch for times when the persons you speak with look embarrassed or appear to get smaller and weaker. Also remember that one defense against shame is rage. Someone who suddenly gets very angry with you may be responding with shame to something you said.

Perhaps you don't shame another who does shame you. Then you are the recipient of shame in a one-way relationship. Even so, be sure to read the next several steps in the guidelines as a way to check out the possibility that you are shaming others more than you know. Then focus your energy on the last few suggestions that concentrate on confronting shame from others.

2. Notice What You Gain Through Shaming Others

One of the reasons a person shames others is simply out of habit. Sometimes shame has become so common that it's used automatically. People may shame others for many additional reasons — a few reasons are the desire for power and control, a wish to feel superior, and as a way to defend against the exposure of their own shame.

I am stronger than you is the sometimes hidden message of those who use shame to gain power and control over another person. He tells her that she is weak, ineffectual, useless, and feeble. He points out her shortcomings as evidence that he should take over control of her life. The messages may be crude. (You're so irresponsible I have to manage our checkbook.) Or they may be subtle. ("Keep trying, dear. One of these days maybe you will be able to handle money. Until then, though, I better write all our checks.")

I am better than you is the hidden message that comes from a shamer who wants to feel superior to her partner or associate. She focuses upon the other's personal or cultural "shortcomings." For instance, she might tell her partner that he is too crude, uneducated, or simplistic ever to be her equal. This person shames others so she can continue to feel specially gifted. She uses shame to maintain her prestige.

Better you than me is usually the secret thought of a person who shames others so that they can't shame him. This defensive maneuver is common in two-way shaming relationships in which shame contests occur often. The idea is to get in the first punch. For example, if a woman can attack her husband for his laziness before he can assail her eating habits, she protects against the exposure of her shame.

Shame can help keep someone powerful, prestigious, and safe. Why, then, would a person choose voluntarily to relinquish this excellent weapon? Indeed, some individuals refuse to quit shaming others. They prefer domination over intimacy. They would view treating others with respect and dignity as a sign of weakness.

We suggest that most people who quit shaming others do so for a selfish reason. They recognize that they can't heal their own shame by pretending that they are somehow stronger, wiser, or better than everybody else. They find that they can only move toward the principles of humanity, humility, competence, and autonomy by giving up their claims to inherent superiority and inferiority. They can't find their place in the human community until they allow the people they love to be human and good enough.

Individuals who want to develop nonshaming relationships with others must take a good look at what they have gained through shaming others. Then, with this knowledge, they can decide whether or not they want to change their behavior.

3. Notice What Damage Occurs to Yourself and Others Through Your Shaming Behavior

Shame attacks hurt the people we care about. Now is the time to pay careful attention to this damage. Do your children stumble to their rooms and refuse to come out, even to play, after you shame them? Does your partner look embarrassed whenever you hammer away at some topic better left alone? Do your work associates flinch at your savage attacks on their personalities?

It takes no great skill to harm another individual through shame. Anybody can do it. Most people are vulnerable to shame because they need approval from the important persons in their lives. We believe that it takes more skill to refrain from shaming others and, instead, to demonstrate consistent caring and appreciation.

Be specific here. Listen to the difference between these two statements:

- "I guess I hurt her with my shame. I must have, but I don't know how."

- "When I told her she was stupid, I could see the pain in her face — the way she blinked her eyes and dropped her head."

Notice that the second comment provides exact cues for the shamer. From now on, he can remind himself that he doesn't want to say or do things that cause that response in another. And, if he does notice someone respond that way, he'll be able to tell himself that he may have tapped that person's shame. He can then choose to change his actions before more damage is done.

The shamer should also attend to the damage he does to himself. Does he feel worse instead of better after a shame attack? Does he feel isolated and alone? Does he invite others to shame him, starting a shame contest? Does he feel less than fully human when he shames others? Does he feel guilty? Here, too, he needs to be as specific as possible. Vague responses are not useful because they do not lead to real behavioral changes.

Warning: Do not rush to make everything right all at once. You may be overwhelmed with shame and guilt if you do. Take your time. Learn about yourself. Start slow and easy. Give yourself time to make real changes in your life.

4. Connect Your Shaming Behavior with Your Own Shame And Self-Hatred Issues

Many habitual shamers are people who are themselves deeply ashamed and full of self-hatred. Furthermore, they often shame others with statements they really believe about themselves. For example, a worker who calls her co-worker boring and dull may secretly believe that she — herself — is boring and dull. This person "projects" her shame outside of herself — she gives it away so she won't feel defective.

It's important to consider this possibility when you study how you shame others. Pay attention in particular to statements that you use most frequently — those are the ones you most likely believe about yourself. Also, look for shaming statements that don't fit the other person at all, such as calling someone lazy who obviously is not. Here again, you may be tapping your own projected shame.

This doesn't mean that every nasty comment you make is about your shame, nor can you assume that all the shaming statements people direct at you are projections of their own shame. There are many reasons that people shame each other.

Shaming another may hide a person's shame from us, but it can't heal our shame. We must have the courage to face our shame, rather than trying to give it away by blaming and attacking another. The next step after awareness is to make a commitment to quit shaming others with our own self-hatred.

5. Make a Commitment to Quit Shaming Others, Regardless of Their Behavior Toward You

We believe that shaming another human being damages the inner dignity of the shamer. The individual who attacks others moves away from her own humanity, humility, autonomy, and competence. Shaming others, in the long run, increases a person's shame instead of lessening it. The person who wants to relieve her own shame needs to make a serious commitment to refrain from shaming others.

"I agree that I should stop shaming my spouse, but what if he keeps on shaming me? I will only agree to quit if he does." This person gives responsibility for her decisions to her husband. She allows him to decide how she will run her life. If he agrees to the truce and reneges, she would have an excuse to return to her own shaming activities.

The point is that we can't wait for the world to become a nicer place. We can't wait until everybody else quits shaming us before we make a serious commitment to change our behavior. Self-determination means we are responsible for our own behavior. The time to stop shaming the people we care about is as soon as we realize that belittling them only diminishes ourselves.

If you habitually tell someone she is fat and ugly, today make a commitment to erase that phrase from your vocabulary. Don't allow yourself to nitpick somebody's tiny failings. Decide today that you will no longer publicly humiliate your partner. Then keep those commitments. Don't *try* not to shame others — *just don't shame them*. If you do break this promise, don't attack yourself. Instead, immediately correct the situation by apologizing to the person you shamed and renewing your promise not to shame others. Remember also to watch and manage your nonverbal behavior so that you don't shame another with a dirty look.

Sometimes, others will respond positively to your changes. They might stop shaming you now that you are no longer degrading them. Try to consider those changes as wonderful bonuses but not as the payoff for your decision. The real reward for not shaming others is that you gain greater self-respect. People who refuse to shame others are less likely to shame themselves.

6. Replace Shaming Behavior
With Respectful Actions Toward Others

People create communication vacuums when they stop one kind of behavior but do not replace it with another. For example, one couple agreed to quit shaming each other after realizing the damage they were doing to the relationship. But then they found they had nothing to talk about. Their partnership was so shame-based that it was virtually empty in the absence of continuous mutual criticism.

Praise, respect, and appreciation are positive ways to replace shaming words and actions. These new behaviors may be difficult at first for the habitual shamer. Many persons will have to make a conscious effort to learn how to speak in a nonshaming manner. First, they will need to pay attention to the good things, instead of the flaws, about others. Second, they will have to learn how to tell others that they respect and appreciate them. Last, they need to resist the urge to praise with condemnation, which returns them to the shaming behavior.

Here are a few ideas to remember if you accept the goal of learning to speak in nonshaming ways:

- Begin each day with a renewed commitment to respect the dignity of others.
- Consciously notice the positive words and actions of the people you care for.
- Look for the inner goodness of each person in your life. Respect is based upon an appreciation of others as human beings, regardless of their specific behaviors.
- Tell others that they are good, good enough, lovable, and important. Don't let the words get stuck in your throat.
- Never use praise to prepare the ground for criticism ("I sure liked the way you cooked dinner tonight, but...").
- You can respect people and still disagree with them. Some conflict is inevitable in a relationship, but that is no excuse for shaming behaviors.
- Don't expect or demand praise in return when you express your appreciation. You might not get it. Don't use that as a justification to attack.
- Pay attention to the changes that occur inside you when you substitute respect for shame. Remember that you are the ultimate beneficiary of this new behavior. Respecting others eventually will increase your own self-respect.

7. Notice How You Are Shamed By Significant Others And the Damage Done

Once you have made a commitment to respect others, you are ready to pay serious attention to how others shame you. This does not mean that you have to be perfect or that you will never shame another individual again. That is impossible.

The point is, you can't realistically expect another person to quit shaming you until you have altered your own shaming behavior.

Begin with a current relationship in which you suspect that you are shamed frequently. Take a few days or a week simply to study the shaming patterns that occur. Don't forget to notice how you shame the other individual as well as how that person shames you.

Watch carefully for repeated phrases and actions — shaming habits that have developed, such as one person condescendingly patting the other on the head or regularly ignoring what the other says. Notice both subtle and crude attacks on your self-esteem. Watch for times when someone seems to deliberately shame you, in contrast to occasions when shaming seems to happen less consciously. You may even notice times when you feel ashamed by messages that may have been intended to make you feel better. Try to remember that, in many relationships, shame is more often dealt out accidentally than with the desire to inflict permanent damage.

A message or action is shaming, regardless of the intent of the sender, when the recipient feels less human, less humble (in the sense of being no better or worse than others), less autonomous, or less competent. It is important that you learn how another person's shaming messages harm you.

- Do I feel somehow dirty or unclean after conversations with a particular individual?
- Do I feel less intelligent or competent than I did before the discussion?
- Do I sense that this person can't accept me unless I give up my independence and do exactly what he or she wants?
- Do I feel small and childlike on a regular basis in the presence of this person?
- Does this person talk about my inadequacies and shortcomings quite often?

Answering these questions helps identify the immediate effects of shame. But it is also necessary to attend to long-term consequences. Ask yourself a few more questions that focus on at least the last several months in your relationship with another individual.

- Overall, how has this person helped me feel that I am a worthwhile human being?
- How has this person diminished my sense of self-worth?
- Does this relationship nurture my inner strength or feed my weaknesses?
- What about this connection decreases or increases my shame?
- Is this relationship moving toward or away from mutual respect?
- Does my life seem more or less meaningful now than before, and how does that connect with this relationship?

Shame causes damage. Your task here is to become more aware of how you are being damaged by shame directed at you. Be specific, just as you were when you assessed how you damaged others with your own shaming behavior. Try not to minimize or exaggerate — just be as accurate as you can. You will soon need to speak clearly to the person who is shaming you, as you confront and challenge shaming behaviors.

8. Confront and Challenge Shaming Behavior Directed Toward You

Now we have reached the decision point. Do we proceed, with all the knowledge we've gathered, to confront the people who shame us? Do we dare risk their denial, anger, defensiveness, and their ability to shame us all the more, in order to gain respectful and appreciative treatment? Are we willing to face the fears of abandonment — fears that reflect our doubts about our own validity as human beings?

It's scary to challenge someone who has the power to shame you. However, the longer shaming continues uncontested, the more damage it does to the receiver. Shame, unchallenged, works its way into the core of an individual's self-concept. Sooner or later, a person who wants to feel healthy pride and dignity will have to confront those who shame her. She will need to tell those people that she is no longer willing to participate in relationships that add to her sense of shame. She will request specific changes in the words and actions of those individuals to promote respect, rather than shame.

Here are a few suggestions if you do decide to confront shaming behavior:

- Be firm and clear about your purpose — know exactly what you want from the other person.
- Be prepared to offer specific examples of behavior that triggered your shame.
- Model respectful behavior both toward yourself and others during the confrontation — above all, do not shame anyone.
- Don't back down in the face of another's immediate defensiveness, hurt, or threats.
- Remember that the goal is not to punish, but to encourage the other person to alter his or her current and future behavior.
- Expect gradual change over a long period of time, rather than immediate success.
- Realize that you will probably need to have several conversations with the other person before you both understand the issue completely.
- Be prepared to deal with the topic of how you shame the person who shames you.

Perhaps these ideas sound complicated. Actually, only one act stands out as a necessity. *Somehow, you must inform the persons who regularly shame you that you will no longer accept that behavior.* Shame makes a person sick. It is time to insist that the important persons in your life contribute to your health instead.

9. Consider Leaving Relationships That Remain Shame-Based

Shaming habits are hard to break, even when both individuals want to quit shaming each other. They are even more difficult to alter when one or both continue shaming the other. This means that the person who challenges a shame-based relationship may need to leave that relationship if the shaming continues unabated.

Shamed persons may dread the idea of leaving a partner (employer, friendship) who shames them. They fear that no one else will ever want them. Sadly, they are paralyzed by the very shame they can't imagine escaping. They have lost faith that they deserve a good place in the world.

No other person should tell you to leave a shaming relationship. Those decisions are too personal and vital for others to judge from afar. But it is reasonable to ask someone what he or she hopes to gain by staying in a relationship. It may be time to get out if the answer to this question is more shame, blame, and unhappiness.

Some shame-based relationships cannot be salvaged. Shame permeates and controls so many interactions that change is impossible. Furthermore, some people seem incapable of, or uninterested in, learning and practicing respectful communication. These relationships may eventually have to be ended in order to develop self-respect.

10. Make and Keep a Commitment to Nurture Nonshaming Relationships

Those who confront shaming behavior in their current relationships will discover that the shame episodes gradually diminish. First, they shame others less frequently. Second, they accept fewer shame attacks from others. Third, they will probably notice that they are more attracted to others who practice respect rather than shame.

Mutually nonshaming relationships must be nurtured. They consist of people who consciously choose to treat each other with dignity and respect. All parties need the courage to confront shaming behavior as it occurs so it can be changed before much damage is done. Above all, individuals in respectful relationships must remember that their partners, friends, and associates deserve to be treated with fairness.

Mutually respectful relationships help heal the wounds of shame. They are only possible when the participants make and regularly renew their vow to refrain from shaming each other. They are sustained through commitment, communication, and sometimes hard work.

Stick with the Winners is a slogan often repeated in self-help communities such as Alcoholics Anonymous. We want to offer the same suggestion. Here the winners are people who treat each other and themselves with honor, respect, and dignity. These are persons who choose not to shame each other.

Summary

Shame in current relationships can be healed. The process begins with checking out how we shame others. You may then decide to convert your shaming into nonshaming behavior. The next major step is to confront and challenge others whose shaming attacks damage you.

People who are shamed regularly have difficulty feeling good about themselves. Therefore, a goal is to develop and maintain mutually respectful relationships. While these relationships may have been deeply shaming, we believe such relationships can be altered — provided both members want change, or at least one of them refuses to continue living with shame. But some relationships are incapable of a pattern of mutual respect. In such cases, you may choose to leave the association in order to protect your self-worth.

EXERCISES

Exercise One

List on a separate sheet of paper the main ways you shame others.

Next, circle any of the following items that you gain as a result of shaming others. List any others you think of.

Feel I'm in control	Stops inner criticism	Pleasure
Get to share misery	Don't have to do things	Get revenge
Get tension release	Get the last word	Get to be right
Get to be best	Stops their criticism	Safe distance
Get to be selfish	Know I'm superior	Feel powerful
Physical power	Get to be angry	Get what I want
Don't have to feel	Get to complain	

Put an "x" before the items on the following list that you lose from shaming others. Put an "o" by the items that others lose when you shame them.

Confidence	Love	Closeness
Pride	Peace of mind	Respect
Self-respect	Companionship	Trust
Spontaneity	Dignity	Playfulness

Specifically, how do you see that others are damaged when you shame them?

Exercise Two

Parents who are ashamed of their youthful "wildness" may shame their children by accusing them of sexual behavior without much justification. Children who have just violated a rule may shame their little brother or sister for being bad when they have done nothing. Partners "project" like this, too, shaming each other because they are seeing their own flaws. Make a list now of everything you shame in others that are also flaws you see in yourself. Be honest!

Exercise Three

Using the following form (on a separate sheet of paper), make a commitment to stop specific shaming behaviors. Any violation of these commitments means you owe the other person an apology, *no matter how that person behaved toward you.* Your commitment is to gain dignity and self-respect due to your own behavior.

Person:

How I shame him or her:

My commitment to stop shaming this person:

Date: Signature:

Results at one day:

Results at one week:

Results at two weeks:

Results at three weeks:

Results at one month:

Results at six weeks:

Exercise Four

Now you are ready to consider how others shame you. Choose just one to start with — this could be a partner, parent, child, sibling, employer, colleague, or counselor. Write on a sheet of paper the shaming messages directed at you. Remember those messages that say *you are not good, not good enough, not lovable, don't belong,* and *should not exist.* These messages

can be transmitted to you verbally or nonverbally. Your sheet of paper should look like this:
Message:

How Received:

Choose one shaming behavior to challenge first. As you see the results, you may wish to challenge other messages. Be clear, specific, and respectful in your challenges. Be sure to use the guidelines noted in the section on confronting and challenging shaming behavior directed toward you (pages 174-175). Respond to this exercise on a separate sheet of paper.

- Shaming message I get now:
- Nonshaming message I want to get instead:
- Two things I will say or do during this conversation:
- Two things I will not say or do during this conversation:
- If the person I confront gets defensive, I will:
- If the person I confront apologizes, I will:
- No matter what, I will:
- No matter what, I will not:

CHAPTER FOURTEEN

Healing the Wounds of Self-Inflicted Shame

"Thoughts that I am worthless and useless still come back — more often than I want to admit. I just don't get too excited about them anymore. The more I respect myself, the less power my shame has over me."

* * * * * * * * *

He always used to think of himself as a "throwaway." Now he knows that he is definitely a "keeper." He has begun appreciating himself. Furthermore, he treats himself with more respect. He has finally realized that a person who wants to enjoy life cannot be filled with disgust and self-hatred.

* * * * * * * * *

"I was completely isolated. I felt disconnected from my family, God, the whole world, and from myself. I had no idea why I was alive. My shame was all I had left. Finally, I went back to my roots in order to put meaning into my life. Once I found my spiritual center, my shame started to let up."

* * * * * * * * *

She believed she could never quit shaming herself. Even after years of therapy, she felt waves of self-hatred and contempt. Then one day she awakened with a simple thought: *It's good to be alive today.* She allowed herself to celebrate her life. For that moment, she could accept herself and appreciate the miracle of her being.

* * * * * * * * * *

If necessary, make a quick review of the general guidelines for healing shame from Chapters Eleven and Twelve (pages 132 and 147) before launching into this chapter. Many of those ideas are quite important here, such as being patient with yourself, accepting your shame as part of the human condition, asking for help, challenging the shame, and taking mental and physical action to alleviate shame. The guidelines here are meant to complement the general guidelines.

GUIDELINES FOR HEALING SELF-SHAMING THOUGHTS AND ACTIONS

1. Notice the condemning messages that seem to appear automatically.
2. Challenge those thoughts and replace them with affirmations.
3. Treat yourself with respect.
4. Celebrate your existence.
5. Develop positive metaphors and symbols for your life.
6. Renew or develop your spiritual life to help find positive meaning for your existence.

1. Notice the Condemning Messages That Seem to Appear Automatically

We may be telling ourselves repeatedly that we are not as good as others. This may be obvious, if we continually apologize or assume what we say makes no sense to anyone else. Our self-shame may also be hidden from view, consisting mostly of insulting or discounting ourselves. Many people focus on a few statements that appear quite frequently and "automatically." These messages symbolize their shame. A few examples are

- *I never do anything right.*
- *Nobody could really love me.*
- *There is something wrong with me.*
- *I am just a nothing.*

Your patience will be needed here. Your first task in halting self-shame is to become fully aware how you condemn yourself. This means paying attention to your thoughts that automatically appear without examination. This means not rushing to alter them so quickly that you fail to appreciate their strength and persistence. Remember, we must learn how to sit quietly with our shame before we can hope to build a new life.

We need to become objective observers of our condition. We must study ourselves and answer questions like these:

- *What do I think or say out loud most often about myself that increases my sense of shame?*
- *What am I doing when I hear these self-condemnations?*
- *What happens to me after I think these thoughts? How do they affect my feelings and behavior?*
- *How convinced am I that these thoughts are accurate?*
- *When did I decide these thoughts were true?*

We may have trouble initiating or completing this task. One reason for this is that shame may have lessened our interest and excitement. It is hard to be curious about ourselves if we feel dull and boring. Another reason might be that we believe we are so bad that we want nothing to do with ourselves. Or we might fear that noticing our shame will only make it worse. Each of these reasons is valid. Each of us has the right to choose where, how, when, and if ever we will begin.

Nevertheless, if we want to minimize the damage from our self-shaming thoughts and behavior, we need to take the time and effort to answer these questions. It is important that, as we do this, we do not add to our shame by blaming ourselves for having self-shaming thoughts. For instance, we should try not to say something like this: *Damn it, there I go again. Another shaming thought. There must really be something wrong with me. I must be sick.*

Instead, recognize that now you are gaining valuable information through these thoughts. You are discovering how you condemn yourself so that, soon, you can begin to challenge those thoughts and increase your self-respect.

2. Challenge Those Thoughts And Replace Them With Affirmations

You begin dialogue with yourself when you challenge your self-shaming statements.

Fortunately, each message guides you toward an affirmation that can help heal the shame. These positive messages will usually be as simple and obvious as the condemnations. For example, the challenge to the shaming statement *I never do anything right* is *I can do things right.* Similarly, *Nobody could really love me* converts to *I am lovable,* while *There is something wrong with me* can be challenged with *There is nothing wrong with me* or *There is something right with me.* Finally, the shaming statement *I am just a nothing (or nobody)* converts to *I am something (or somebody).*

No one message heals all shame because each person's shame is unique. That is why, if our lives are shame-based, we need to identify our own affirmations. These affirmations should be clear and simple. They must directly challenge the one or two most significant shaming messages. They must also be at least a little believable when we say them to ourselves.

Imagine a conversation that could take place inside your head. It might sound something like this:

Shamed Self: *I know that there is something wrong with me. I've known that for years.*

Respectful Self: *I'm getting tired of hearing you say that. I've decided that there is something right with me.*

Shamed Self: *Nonsense. I'm broken, damaged, useless, worthless. . . .*

Respectful Self: *I'm human. There is something right with me.*

You may not win this battle. The important thing is that you are actually challenging your shame instead of allowing it to run your life. You are disputing the shaming messages that may have gone unquestioned for years.

Notice the assumptions you make about the value of your being. "Facts" are not necessarily of much use, since you do not have to prove there is something right with you by citing good deeds, pure thoughts, or accomplishments. *There is something right with you because you want there to be something right.* Recovery from excessive shame is partly a matter of decision.

Your intellect and reason certainly are important in healing excessive shame. They prepare for the dialogue that heals shame. But intellect and reason alone cannot produce major changes in your basic assumption about your identity. They alone cannot give you a reason for being nor put meaning into your life. You need to be able to say to yourself: *I exist and I am good.* You must decide to have faith in yourself and your world.

3. Treat Yourself with Respect

The Alcoholics Anonymous community has developed the idea of Act As If thinking and behavior. The newly recovering person, still uncertain about a commitment to abstinence, is asked to Act As If he really wanted to stay sober. He then acts in a fully committed manner, doing such things as attending AA meetings rather than spending time in taverns. Many times, the person who starts out acting as if he wanted sobriety eventually grows to value this behavior. His body and mind respond so well that he eventually cherishes his abstinence and no longer needs to drink.

You may also need to begin recovery from self-shaming with Act As If thinking and behavior. Specifically, you may have to ask yourself, *What would I do now if I truly respected myself?*

Don't wait until you feel free from excessive shame to begin treating yourself respectfully. Instead, start immediately to retrain yourself in the habits of healthy pride, dignity, and honor. That means you can substitute self-caring thoughts and behaviors for self-shaming ones whenever possible.

You may need to ask others for help in order to learn what self-respecting behaviors are. You need to model your actions on what others who seem to honor themselves do. You might even speak directly to those persons. They may be able to share their own experiences — how they have learned to care for themselves. Some of them may also have had to practice Acting As If thinking for a while.

4. Celebrate Your Existence

The celebration can be a simple one. It is private and personal. Mostly, it consists of reminding yourself every day to appreciate and enjoy life.

The opposite of celebrating your existence is apologizing for it, something that many persons who feel deeply shamed do.

You can begin or renew this celebration remembering the four principles:

1. humanity,
2. humility,
3. competence,
4. autonomy.

These principles can encourage you to recognize that you are no better or worse than others, that you are capable and unique.

I am who I am is the statement of a person who has learned to accept himself. There is no apology for being, no focus on weaknesses, deficits, failures, or shortcomings. Nor is there narcissism (which may include conceit and excessive pride) or grandiosity.

Since "facts" may not be enough to convince us that we belong on this planet, we must look for deeper faith and conviction. No one can really justify their presence on earth with arguments about how much good they do, beauty they create, or money they make. We must decide to celebrate our existence rather than how we live and what we do.

One reminder: continuing shame can sometimes signal the presence of biochemically-induced depression. Joylessness often is a part of depression. If the tasks in this section of the book seem impossible for you even to imagine doing, you may need to review the signs of depression (Exercise Two, pages 70-71).

5. Develop Positive Metaphors and Symbols for Your Life

Certain images occur regularly with shame. There is the stooped-over man with head bent down or the blushing woman covering her face with her hands. These pictures reflect a physical and emotional response to shame. Each person probably develops a specific image of shame unique to him- or herself. For one person, it might be a vivid memory from childhood of a parent pointing a finger down at her. Another person might picture her shame as a pathetic, weak figure unable to do anything well. Yet another might remember a particularly embarrassing scene, such as becoming "stinking drunk," as the symbol of his shame. These vivid portraits both reflect and add to shame. The portraits reflect it by showing people how they look when they are ashamed. The portraits add to these people's shame by diminishing their sense of self-worth.

These "automatic" images accompany automatic shaming thoughts.

Pride, honor, dignity, and *self-respect* are words that produce very different mental visions. Think of yourself as standing upright, looking straight ahead, full of grace and strength. These positive images are vital. If you want to heal from excessive shame, you will need to develop several positive pictures of yourself to counter habitual self-shaming images.

The best images are those that occur naturally. These originate from actual successes in your life or from idealized concepts of yourself. They will feel right to you. You will sense that you are seeing yourself at your best — as a good person in a good world — when you allow yourself to develop these images.

Some pictures of your nonshamed, healthy self may come from childhood. For instance, a man might remember a scene where he and his father are walking down a trail together during hunting season. They are talking "man to man," not really caring about the hunt, just enjoying each other's company because of their mutual interest in, and respect for, each other. The key ingredients in this scene are its clarity, simplicity, and power. The now grown man can still use this image to remind him that he can live with dignity.

Other images may be more immediate. A woman who has, in the past, been dominated by men may be able to visualize herself calmly and articulately explaining her ideas to her boyfriend or male employer. This picture will assist her in her real encounters with men, because she will not begin with the assumption that she is inadequate.

Not all positive images have to be as concrete as the ones above. You might identify with something you believe has inner dignity, such as an eagle or oak tree. You might try to do things every day that reflect that dignity.

- *If I were like an eagle, I would not gossip about others or listen to their gossip.*
- *If I were like an oak tree, I would keep my head up even in the bad times.*

Please note that your images do not have to be heroic. You do not have to imagine yourself as a conquering hero destroying everything in your path to relieve shame. In fact, such heroic images may lead to greater shame when you realize that you cannot live up to them. The portraits that relieve excessive shame are those that help you feel good about being you. They are not fantasies about who you can never be.

Do you need help developing respectful images of yourself? The exercises at the end of this chapter can help with this task.

6. Renew or Develop Your Spiritual Life to Help Find Positive Meaning for Your Existence

You can continue your recovery process by recognizing that you need to mend your damaged spirit as well as your feelings, thoughts, and actions. You may need to renew or develop your spirituality through prayer, meditation, and discussion with others.

This spiritual search may be scary. Sometimes shamed persons tremble at the thought of renewing contact with a Higher Power that they believed condemned them long ago. Others lost interest in spirituality as part of their general loss of heart and hope. Still others may have to deal with their rage at a God they think allowed them to feel so badly for so long. Finally, there are those who have little interest in organized religion, and who do not wish to connect their deep shame with spiritual distress. They may fear that they will have to embrace an uncomfortable religion.

We will make no effort to direct your spiritual search. All we are suggesting is that you need to move past the isolation and desolation of shame, and move toward making connection with the universe. We must somehow find our spirit and a deep sense that our lives have meaning.

Shame separates us from the world. When we heal, we will discover that we are not alone. Some people discover their fears of abandonment ease when they gain the conviction that they are firmly held in the hands of a loving God. Others simply rejoice in a private but profound recognition that they have an inner spiritual light.

Some authors write that shame (normal, healthy shame) helps preserve and protect spirituality. They note that deeply spiritual events in a person's life are often private and personal — certainly, few persons would want to have their prayers and meditations made public. This idea reminds us that *the goal is not to eliminate shame but to learn how to appreciate and use it appropriately.* The person who locates a spiritual center will not be without shame, but he or she will be free from excessive shame and open to the normal shame that maintains inner harmony.

Summary

We have a remarkable ability to harm ourselves. One way we do this is by shaming ourselves. When we emphasize our weaknesses and shortcomings, we forget that we are inherently valuable and worthwhile. In this chapter, we have provided guidelines designed to help change self-shaming thoughts and actions into self-respect.

Some of the guidelines are directed at the shaming messages we repeat to ourselves. These messages prevent us from developing a more positive viewpoint. They must be noticed, challenged, and replaced with positive affirmations. We must also change our behavior so we consistently treat ourselves with respect.

Two signs of recovery are when we learn to celebrate our existence and when we develop positive metaphors and symbols for our life.

Spiritual emptiness and despair must also be addressed. As deeply shamed persons, we may have lost our faith that life has meaning. We need to begin or renew our spiritual search so we can find a place for ourselves in the world.

EXERCISES

Exercise One

Return to Chapter One, Exercise Three (page 19) for a brief review. If some of these condemning messages are a problem for you, try the following exercise, using a separate sheet of paper.

- Shame message I give myself:
- What am I doing when I give myself this message?
- Where or from whom did I learn this message?
- How old was I when I decided the message was true?
- What positive decision do I need to make to change the message?

Write affirmations that will help you put the past behind you — affirmations that reflect the new decision you are making about who you are. Now, repeating these affirmations often, begin Acting As If they are true. For example, if you have decided that you are beautiful rather than ugly, treat yourself that way and Act As If you are. If you have decided that you are smart rather than an idiot, listen to your thoughts and opinions carefully. Tell yourself they are worthwhile. And act with others as if you are proud of what you think and say. Note the results of Acting As If on a separate sheet of paper.

Exercise Two

Pride, honor, self-respect, and dignity are the antidotes to self-shaming behavior. Make a list (on a separate sheet of paper) of times you treated yourself nonshamefully. For example:

- I felt *pride* (satisfaction in something I did) when:
- I felt *honorable* (I acted with honesty and integrity) when:
- I felt *self-respect* (I was kind and considerate of myself) when:
- I felt *dignified* (worthwhile, able to hold my head up) when:

What do you need to do to have more of these experiences?

Exercise Three

We celebrate our existence when we do something just for ourselves instead of only for others. For example, we celebrate our existence by

- taking a walk and experiencing a sense of belonging in nature, and
- letting in another's love, by dancing or singing, by writing a poem expressing our feelings, and by deciding to allow ourselves to be happy and free.

Those of us who have acted arrogantly can celebrate our life by focusing on our humility and humanity. People who are shame-deficient can celebrate by honoring the lives of others as well as their own. Celebrate your life in at least one special way this week. If this seems foreign, maybe a friend can help you learn how to take pleasure in being alive. List several possibilities.

Exercise Four

Give yourself at least half an hour and go for a walk. Let yourself wander, rather than going to a specific place. As you stroll slowly, allow something positive in nature to come to your attention — a unique bush, a special tree. a brook, a nesting bird. When something like this pops out at you, look at its quality and beauty. Discover the message it has for you, and consider ways you may be similar to it. Use it to keep a positive image of yourself this week. Write on a separate sheet of paper what you learned from it. (Example: one impatient man learned from oak trees that the patience to grow slowly can equal strength.)

Exercise Five

Strong shame experiences and self-shaming can empty our life of meaning. We get confused about why we are alive, what use we are, and whether there is any future for us. We must reconnect to the world. One way is to focus on our breathing, making it deeper and more relaxed, and allowing the extra oxygen we take in to inspire us. Often, those of us who have been continually shamed begin to unconsciously hold our breath — this makes us even more frightened, depressed, and disconnected than we already are. So spending a few minutes breathing deeply whenever we find ourselves holding our breath or feeling depressed is a good start at reconnecting — it puts us back in touch with ourselves.

Answer the following questions on a separate sheet of paper.

- What do you notice about your breathing this week?
- How does breathing more deeply on a regular basis change your relationship to the world?

Self-discovery or spiritual reconnection also means regularly practicing some form of relaxed meditation, prayer, or spiritual visualization (for example, visualizing a Higher Power).

- The Society of Friends (Quakers) says, "There is that of God in each of us." Answer on a separate sheet of paper how this applies to you.

CHAPTER FIFTEEN

Help for the Shame-Deficient Person

She had felt special and gifted all her life. Aloof and superior, she calmly waited for the world to acknowledge her obvious excellence. Now she realizes that she is simply human. She is finally climbing down from her throne.

* * * * * * * * *

"I was part of the 'let it all hang out' movement of the sixties and seventies. I was uninhibited in everything I did. Back then, I thought you had to sacrifice dignity in order to be real."

* * * * * * * * *

"My family was crude. We talked about everything. Now I have to be very careful not to embarrass myself and my associates when I speak. I've had to learn to respect their boundaries."

* * * * * * * * *

The last several chapters have focused on the problems of persons with normal or excessive amounts of shame and how healing from shame can be accomplished. Here we will look at what can be done if you have too little shame and tend to be self-centered, immodest, and indiscreet.

Shame deficiency does not have to be extreme. Probably everyone has had a time when his or her ego inflated to the point of losing contact with the world. For instance, a person is asked at a party to tell others about a recent accomplishment. He starts to do so, feels wonderful, gets carried away, and then notices about ten minutes later that everyone has quit paying attention. The person with normal shame will feel humbled by this experience. It is hoped he can take it in stride and perhaps even see the humor in the situation. The excessively shamed person will see this event as more proof that he is defective, not realizing that it happens to almost everybody sooner or later. The very shame-deficient person may not even notice that others have quit listening and will continue his monologue indefinitely.

Normal shame disconnects one person from another but provides hope that the connection can be reestablished. But the shame-deficient person may not even recognize that the connection has been broken. The shame-deficient person is so full of herself that she assumes people are always interested in her words and actions. She also lacks empathy for others. She cannot place herself in the shoes of those around her because she never thinks to take her own shoes off.

We have discussed the idea of *recovery* from excessive shame. In shame deficiency, the issue is more one of *discovery*. The shame-deficient person must try to discover the value of normal shame, discretion, respect, and personal dignity. He must sacrifice his self-perceived position as the center of the universe in order to join the human race.

The following guidelines might help shame-deficient people in this discovery process.

GUIDELINES FOR RELIEVING SHAME DEFICIENCY

1. Accept the principle of humility — that you are no better or worse than others.
2. Develop interest and concern for others.
3. Practice privacy and modesty to counter immodesty.
4. Practice tact and respect for others.

1. Accept the Principle of Humility — That You Are No Better or Worse Than Others

The self-centered, narcissistic person who lacks normal shame must make an important decision. Does she want to cling to her idea that she is somehow special, definitely better than those around her? Or is she willing to give up that concept and embrace the principle of humility? This is no easy choice. Indeed, many persons attempt to compromise. They practice "false modesty," pretending to be just like everybody else. But secretly they still think they are superior.

It is hard to alter the basic assumptions we make about life. The person who has always "just known" that he is superior may experience tremendous confusion when he discovers that there is no basis for his belief. He may continue to insist that he is smarter, wiser, et cetera. For that matter, all of us can find at least a few reasons to justify our supremacy. The shame-deficient person concentrates on these points to validate, to himself, his natural excellence. He feels he would be nothing at all if he were not superior.

This sense of nothingness is the greatest problem. Certain people cannot move toward humility because they confuse it with nothingness. They have always been at the center of their universe. It is like asking the sun to agree to become a small planet. The shame-deficient person may feel life is not possible under such conditions.

The first step for healing, then, is for the shame-deficient person to recognize that humility is possible. This means that she sees clearly that she can learn to accept this idea. It means she can envision herself as a "planet" instead of as a "sun."

The second step occurs when the shame-deficient person decides that he wants to live humbly. But why should he? In order to become emotionally and spiritually reconnected to the rest of humanity. Conceit deprives him of the warmth of community and intimacy. He needs to leave the loneliness of superiority and join the rest of the human race.

The decision is painful. The shame-deficient person may choose to maintain her sense of supremacy because it is familiar, it seems right, or because she prefers it to the nothingness that she feels she would face if she abandoned it. She might also decide to explore the world of humility to learn if trading superiority for community is worth it. She might vacillate from one state to the other frequently in this process.

Humility means the acceptance that you are neither better nor worse than others. It is a philosophy of respect for the inner dignity of all people. The humble individual does not have to give up what he is good at nor pretend that he is "average" at everything he does. He can still pursue excellence in his activities.

Nor should we confuse humility with the word "humiliation." A person can be humble without suffering humiliation from others. The term *humility* implies respect for the self and others; *humiliation* implies disrespect.

A third step in the process of embracing humility is making a sincere and consistent effort to live humbly. This must be more than a nice idea or an interesting possibility. It must be lived daily. Three ways to begin living a more humble life are described in guidelines two, three, and four.

2. Develop Interest and Concern for Others

If you identified some characteristics of shame deficiency in yourself, you need to make a conscious effort to become more interested in other people. It means carefully listening to what others are saying without impatiently trying to redirect their attention to you. It means noticing the inner dignity of each person you meet.

Erving Polster describes in *Every Person's Life Is Worth a Novel* how we could write a story about each person because we all lead interesting and exciting lives. He suggests that many people do not realize the richness and beauty of their experiences. He believes that therapy often consists of a counselor drawing out her client's story so that both can appreciate it better. Deeply shamed people often benefit from this approach. They need someone to help them realize their own grace and beauty.

The shame-deficient person needs to put down the novel of his own life, which he rereads constantly, and get involved with the stories of others. He must learn how to draw others out — to help them tell their tales. For example, the husband who insists on telling his wife about every play he made as his softball team's shortstop may have to remind himself to give a quick summary and then really listen to his wife's concerns.

It is not enough to pretend to hear the other person. The parent who nods her head to her child's words while actually reading the newspaper is still absorbed with herself. We must learn to focus our attention on someone else. We must be willing to become as fascinated with another person as we have been with ourselves.

Each individual has unique wisdom. The shame-deficient person will learn much about life when he lets himself gather experience and knowledge of others. But first he must recognize that he does not know everything. He must humble himself by admitting that the rest of the world does not exist simply to serve him.

Shame-deficient people can learn to shift their attention off themselves and onto others. At first, they may only be able to do so for a few moments at a time. But with regular practice, they will gradually improve this skill. It will help to renew this commitment every morning and even, initially, to keep a record of what you have learned about others each day. Remember that the goal here is not to find out what is bad or defective about others. It is to discover their positive qualities and their inner dignity.

3. Practice Privacy and Modesty to Counter Immodesty

The shame-deficient person needs to practice modesty and privacy to counterbalance the tendency to display himself excessively.

The modest person does not call extra attention to herself. For example, she can stay in the background and let others receive praise. She has a certain reserve that she uses to stay unpretentious. She does not need to tell others everything about herself. Her modesty reflects an inner peace — she knows who she is and has confidence in her value as a human being.

A modest person enjoys some attention and appreciation. Unlike the excessively shamed individual, he does not fear being seen. He can move with grace from foreground to background and is comfortable with himself in either position.

A person needs privacy to maintain a boundary between herself and the world. Normal shame helps us preserve our boundaries by telling us when we have violated someone's privacy, including our own. A shame-deficient person needs her shame so she can become more aware of the difference between herself and others. She needs to see that she cannot know everything about the people around her and that they do not need to know all about her either.

The shame-deficient person must learn to keep a few "secrets." We are not talking about serious matters that lead to unhealthy shame if hidden. The idea is to practice staying in the background at times when you would previously have sought attention. One example is to do something nice for someone else while discussing your generosity with no one. Another would be to sing harmony instead of taking the lead at a songfest. A third example would be to hear a piece of gossip and keep it to yourself. The person who tries these activities may gain a new respect for the value of modesty and privacy.

4. Practice Tact and Respect for Others

Tact and discretion complement modesty and privacy. They remind a person that others can feel shame because of her lack of concern for their boundaries.

Here is what *not* to do:

- Tell everyone you know what you just heard about a friend.
- Announce in public the details of your partner's latest embarrassing episode.
- Tell your friends about your adolescent child's sexual activity.
- Speak loudly in a "private" conversation so that others become unnecessarily aware.

The person who disregards tact shames others. This behavior might be intentional and planned. It might be a half-conscious effort to attack others without taking responsibility for our actions. It might be entirely accidental or a product of ignorance in social affairs. Whatever the reasons, indiscretion signals others that a person has violated the shame boundary.

The shame-deficient person needs to practice tact for two reasons. First, he will gain respect for others. According to Gershen Kaufman, author of *Shame: The Power of Caring,* this will help the shame-deficient person keep the "interpersonal bridge" between him and others open. Second, he will learn more about himself and his own shame as he recognizes the shame of the people he cares for. He will appreciate himself in a different way — as a person who can feel normal shame. That, in turn, can direct him toward good pride, dignity, and self-respect.

Summary

The key to healing shame deficiency is to develop a deep appreciation for the principle of humility — that each of us is no better nor worse than others. True acceptance of this concept, along with a commitment to practice it in our daily affairs, will help the shame-deficient person make better connections with others. He will also begin to feel less isolated, more part of the action than before.

The shame-deficient person must choose between her desire to be special (the center of the universe) and her desire to bond with others. Humility and self-centeredness do not mix. If she chooses humility, the tools she needs include an increased interest and concern for others, an ability to practice privacy and modesty, and an interest in being tactful and respectful of others.

EXERCISES

Exercise One

Those of us who are shame deficient often focus too exclusively on ourselves — *our* opinions, *our* activities, *our* feelings, and *our* desires. In the process, although we think we know other people well, we learn very little about them. Sometimes we fail to notice that there are fascinating differences between people. We need to be interested in others. Choose a person to get to know. Spend time with that person, encouraging him or her to talk, and listen carefully to what is said. Then answer the following questions:

- How old is this person, and where has he or she lived?
- What jobs has this person had?
- What are three main dislikes the person has?
- What are three things he or she likes very much?
- Who does this person share his or her feelings with?
- What is something unusual about this person?

- Is he or she extroverted or introverted? Why?
- How does this person feel about him- or herself?
- How does this person feel about me?

Do this exercise again with at least two other people focusing mostly on them.

Exercise Two

If you are used to getting a lot of attention, take a role in the background on the next project, committee, or activity you are involved in. While you are in the background, make a list of the strengths of others who are currently getting attention. See if you can find any strengths in them that you would like to develop in yourself. If you don't see strengths, try another situation and do this exercise again until you can.

Exercise Three

Refuse to tell secrets or gossip for one week, no matter how much attention or status you could get by repeating what you know, or how knowledgeable you would feel in telling. What did you gain? What did you lose? What did you learn about yourself? What did you learn about others?

Exercise Four

Remember the signs of shame and embarrassment — someone looking down or away, blushing, pulling away. Train yourself to notice these signs in others. Then, if these occur while you are in conversation with someone, ask quietly if you have been tactless. If you are out in public, ask the person if he or she would prefer to discuss the subject privately. If you have trouble with tactlessness, you will have to learn appropriate discretion by asking for information about where the boundaries are. Notice also how you feel when you generate an embarrassed response from someone. Do you feel concerned? Superior? A secret pleasure? Something else? What does this attitude say about your ability to be human? To be humble?

EPILOGUE

Several years ago we began our research on shame. At first, all we found were books and articles full of pessimism. The authors of these volumes seemed to imply that those with chronic shame could not be helped much because shame represents a failure of being. Gradually, however, we discovered writers who noticed the positive value of shame. These men and women were more optimistic because they could see that the outlook for a shamed person was not hopeless.

We believe that shame heals. Certainly shame is a painful condition, but it is also a temporary state. The shamed person feels isolated from others, but hopes to return to the warmth of community. Feelings of shame signal us that something is wrong — that we have become disconnected from ourselves, the people we love, the world, and a spiritual Higher Power. We need to notice our shame so we can learn how once again to lift our heads and become part of the human race.

We have emphasized four principles of living: *humanity, humility, autonomy,* and *competence.* We can focus on these four concepts to relieve our pain. They remind us we are human, we are no better or worse than others, we are unique and independent, and we are "good enough" to deserve a place in this world.

Most of us will need help to heal our shame. Shame mends best when it is brought into the light of nonshaming relationships. We must counter our natural desire to hide our shame by letting others reassure us that we will not be abandoned. We will have to challenge our tendencies to attack and shame ourselves. We may need to challenge others in our life (past or present) who contributed to our shame. All this takes time, energy, courage, and patience. Shame heals, but seldom quickly.

Shame must be replaced rather than just removed. We can replace shame with honor, dignity, self-worth, and realistic pride. We can treat ourselves and others with respect. We can see the beauty and goodness in every human being, including ourselves.

We hope you have gained knowledge through the information we have presented. Even more, we hope that you will use it to help create a world in which shame is accepted without fear or gloom. Most of all, we wish each of you a life that is centered around mutual appreciation and respect.

THE AUTHORS

SELECT BIBLIOGRAPHY

Bradshaw, John. *Healing The Shame That Binds You.* Deerfield Beach, Fla.: Health Communications, Inc., 1988.

Ekman, Paul. *The Face of Man: Expressions of Universal Emotions in a New Guinea Village.* New York: Garland Publishing, Inc., 1980.

Evans, Sue. "Shame, Boundaries, and Dissociation in Chemically Dependent, Abusive and Incestuous Families." In *The Treatment of Shame and Guilt in Alcoholism Counseling,* edited by Ronald T. Potter-Efron and Patricia S. Potter-Efron. New York: Haworth Press, 1988.

Fischer, Bruce. "The Process of Healing Shame." In *The Treatment of Shame and Guilt in Alcoholism Counseling,* edited by Ronald T. Potter-Efron and Patricia S. Potter-Efron. New York: Haworth Press, 1988.

Flanigan, Beverly. "Shame and Forgiving in Alcoholism." In *The Treatment of Shame and Guilt in Alcoholism Counseling,* edited by Ronald T. Potter-Efron and Patricia S. Potter-Efron. New York: Haworth Press, 1988.

Izard, Carroll E. *Face of Emotion.* New York: Appleton-Century-Crofts, 1971.

Kaufman, Gershen. *Shame: The Power of Caring.* 2d ed. Cambridge, Mass.: Schenkman Books, Inc., 1985.

Kinston, Warren. "The Shame of Narcissism." In *The Many Faces of Shame,* edited by Donald L. Nathanson. New York: Guilford Press, 1987.

Kohut, Heinz. *The Search For Self.* New York: International Press, 1978.

Kübler-Ross, Elisabeth. *On Death and Dying.* New York: Macmillan, 1969.

Kurtz, Ernest. *Shame and Guilt: Characteristics of the Dependency Cycle.* Center City Minn.: Hazelden, 1981.

–. *Not-God: A History of Alcoholics Anonymous.* Center City, Minn.: Hazelden, 1979.

Lewis, Helen Block. *Shame and Guilt in Neurosis.* New York: International Universities Press, Inc., 1971.

Morrison, Andrew. "Working with Shame in Psychoanalytic Treatment." *Journal of the American Psychoanalytic Association* 32 (3) (1984): 479-505.

—. "Shame, Ideal Self and Narcissism." *Contemporary Psychoanalysis* 19 (2) (April 1983): 195-318.

Nathanson, Donald L. "A Timetable For Shame." In *The Many Faces of Shame,* edited by Donald L. Nathanson. New York: Guilford Press, 1987.

Piers, Gerhart and Milton Singer. *Shame and Guilt.* Springfield, Ill.: Charles Thomas, 1953.

Polster, Erving. *Every Person's Life Is Worth a Novel.* New York: W. W. Norton, 1987.

Polster, Erving and Miriam Polster. *Gestalt Therapy Integrated: Contours of Theory and Practice.* New York: Vintage, 1973.

Ramsey, Ed. "From Guilt to Shame Through A.A.: A Self-Reconciliation Process." In *The Treatment of Shame and Guilt in Alcoholism Counseling,* edited by Ronald T. Potter-Efron and Patricia S. Potter-Efron. New York: Haworth Press, 1988.

Schneider, Carl. "A Mature Sense of Shame." In *The Many Faces of Shame,* edited by Donald L. Nathanson. New York: Guilford Press, 1987.

—. *Shame, Exposure and Privacy.* Boston: Beacon Press, 1977.

Smalley, Sondra. Lecture on codependency. Eau Claire, Wis., 6 September 1985.

Smedes, Lewis. *Forgive and Forget: Healing the Hurts We Don't Deserve.* New York: Pocket Books, 1984.

Tomkins, Silvan. "Shame." In *The Many Faces of Shame,* edited by Donald L. Nathanson. New York: Guilford Press, 1987.

INDEX

S

HAZELDEN INFORMATION AND EDUCATIONAL SERVICES is a division of the Hazelden Foundation, a not-for-profit organization. Since 1949, Hazelden has been a leader in promoting the dignity and treatment of people afflicted with the disease of chemical dependency.

The mission of the foundation is to improve the quality of life for individuals, families, and communities by providing a national continuum of information, education, and recovery services that are widely accessible; to advance the field through research and training; and to improve our quality and effectiveness through continuous improvement and innovation.

Stemming from that, the mission of this division is to provide quality information and support to people wherever they may be in their personal journey—from education and early intervention, through treatment and recovery, to personal and spiritual growth.

Although our treatment programs do not necessarily use everything Hazelden publishes, our bibliotherapeutic materials support our mission and the Twelve Step philosophy upon which it is based. We encourage your comments and feedback.

The headquarters of the Hazelden Foundation are in Center City, Minnesota. Additional treatment facilities are located in Chicago, Illinois; New York, New York; Plymouth, Minnesota; St. Paul, Minnesota; and West Palm Beach, Florida. At these sites, we provide a continuum of care for men and women of all ages. Our Plymouth facility is designed specifically for youth and families.

For more information on Hazelden, please call **1-800-257-7800**. Or you may access our World Wide Web site on the Internet at **http://www.hazelden.org**.

Other titles that will interest you...

Passages through Recovery
An Action Plan for Preventing Relapse
by Terence T. Gorski

This pioneering work from Terence T. Gorski describes six stages of recovery from chemical dependency and offers sound advice for working through the challenges of each stage. 173 pp.
Order No. 5687   Revised

Of Course You're Angry
by Gayle Rosellini and Mark Worden

Feeling angry is a normal, healthy emotion. Yet learning to express anger appropriately can be difficult. This book looks at many forms of anger such as violence, depression, and manipulation, and offers specific guidelines for learning healthy ways to acknowledge and express anger. 136 pp.
Order No. 5689   Revised

The Presence at the Center
The Twelve Steps and the Journey Deep Within

This moving narrative of a recovering man's spiritual journey provides insight into personal transformation, change, and the joy found in a new way of living. It's a candid account of how the spiritual lessons taught in the Twelve Steps can lead to unexpected new beginnings, directions, and freedom. 80 pp.
Order No. 1406
